MILAN

Compact Guide: Milan is the ultimate easy-reference guide to Europe's capital of fashion. It tells you all you need to know about Milan's great attractions, from its soaring cathedral to Castello Sforzesco, from La Scala opera house to Da Vinci's *Last Supper*.

This is one of 120 Compact Guides, which combine the interests and enthusiasms of two of the world's best-known information providers: Insight Guides, whose titles have set the standard for visual travel guides since 1970, and Discovery Channel, the world's premier source of non-fiction television programming.

Star Attractions

An instant reference to some of Milan's most popular tourist attractions to help you on your way.

Milan Cathedral p12

Galleria Vittorio Emanuele p25

Teatro alla Scala p26

Museo Poldi-Pezzoli p28

Pinacoteca Brera p33

Castello Sforzesco p42

Santa Maria delle Grazie p53

Leonardo da Vinci's Last Supper p54

Michelangelo's Pietà p47

Northern Italian Lakes p76

Certosa di Pavia p79

Milan

Introduction

Milan – the Secret Capital...5
Historical Highlights 8

Places

Route 1: Milan Cathedral..**12**
Route 2: Palazzo Reale – Galleria Vittorio Emanuele – La Scala **20**
Route 3: Brera – Cimitero Monumentale – Giardini Pubblici.....**31**
Route 4: Castello Sforzesco – Parco Sempione.........................**42**
Route 5: Piazzale Cadorna – Sant'Ambrogio.............................**51**
Route 6: Piazza Borromeo – Ambrosiana – San Satiro..............**58**
Route 7: Piazza Fontana – Santa Maria della Passione –
         La Rotunda...**61**
Route 8: Museo di Milano – Palazzo Serbelloni – Villa Reale ...**66**
Route 9: San Lorenzo Maggiore – Porta Ticinese –
         Sant'Eustorgio – Santa Maria presso San Celso..........**69**
Additional Sights **73**
Excursions:
         Monza..**75**
         Northern Italian Lakes...**76**
         Bergamo **79**
         Certosa di Pavia...**79**
         Pavia...**81**

Culture

Art History **83**
Music, Theatre and Nightlife **87**

Leisure

Food and Drink **89**
Shopping and Markets **92**

Practical Information

Getting There **95**
Getting Around **97**
Facts for the Visitor..**99**
Accommodation..**102**

Index..**104**

Milan – the Secret Capital

The Italians call it their 'secret capital', *la capitale morale*. Milan *(Milano)*, is Italy's second largest city and its main industrial metropolis, the city that not only possesses the country's finest shops and its most spectacular churches, but also some of its ugliest slums. Milan owes its growth and prosperity to its wholly favourable location in the Po Basin; this is where a number of important transalpine roads meet the traffic network of the southern alpine foothills, between the Po, Adda and Ticino rivers. The city's position is reflected in its name, which has its roots in the Latin *Mediolanum* (in the middle of the plain).

In late antiquity, the Roman Empire was partly governed from Milan. In the Middle Ages the city was the springboard for conquests of Italy, and right up to modern times the surrounding plain was the stage on which 'the people of Europe settled their scores by the sword'. Today Milan is a melting-pot for people who have come here in search of work, not only from all parts of Italy, but also from abroad, particularly from the African continent.

Milan is not only one of the largest cities in Italy, but also one of the most lively and elegant. However, since life here has revolved around progress and modernity, and the earning and spending of money, it has acquired the reputation of being a 'non-Italian', rather 'northern' city. However, Milan is far more than just a trading centre with a centuries-old tradition; it is also one of the country's most important cities of art and a significant centre of contemporary culture. Visitors are unlikely to tire of Milan: apart from the sheer inexhaustible choice of shopping, there are also many fine historical sights to see – art collections, churches and palaces – as well as lively cultural events. This noisy, bustling metropolis also contains some delightful and unexpectedly peaceful corners.

The city's environs are also worth closer inspection, since they are home to a multitude of castles and such attractions as Lake Maggiore and Lake Como, the towns of Monza and Bergamo, and the Carthusian monastery at Pavia – all little more than an hour's drive away.

Position and size

Milan lies between 100m–147m (328ft–480ft) above sea level, not far from the River Po and the Alps, on the gently southwards-sloping Po Basin between two small rivers: Olona in the west and Lambro in the east. The city is connected to the Northern Italian lakes and the large rivers of the Po Basin by shipping canals *(navigli)*: to Lake Maggiore by the Naviglio Grande; the Po River by the Naviglio Pavese, and the Adda River and Lake Como by the Naviglio della Martesana.

5

Fashion's capital

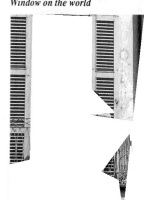

Window on the world

Roof of the Galleria Vittorio Emanuele

The city of Milan covers an area of around 182sq km (70sq miles) and has a circumference of approximately 95km (59 miles). With a population of close to 1.5 million, Milan is the second-largest city in Italy and it occupies 10th place in the European city league. With its 35 suburbs, Greater Milan has a population of 3.78 million (1951: 1.28 million). The population density is 1,900 per sq km.

Climate

Like the whole of the Po Basin, Milan has a continental climate, with fairly harsh winters and hot, muggy summers. The weather can change fairly rapidly, meaning that on any one day, temperature variations can be considerable. The best times to visit are the spring and autumn, when the average temperatures lie between 15–19°C. During the summer months the city bakes in temperatures of around 30°C. Precipitation is generally quite high, and snow often falls in winter. Like many other areas of the Po Plain, Milan can also get very misty during winter, with fogs lasting up to two or three weeks.

Milan is a flagship city

Administration

Milan is the capital of the province of the same name and also the capital of the Italian region of Lombardy. The city is the seat of an archbishop, a court of appeal, higher transport and financial authorities, countless chambers of commerce and consulates. It has three universities (state, Catholic and commercial, with the country's most important business school, Bocconi), a polytechnic and academies of music and art.

Economy

Milan is Italy's most important industrial and commercial city as well as being the country's centre of banking and publishing. The most important sectors are steel, chemicals, textiles, construction and computer services. Milan also is famous for its production of furniture and gold jewellery; the city is a metropolis of fashion and modern industrial design.

The Po Plain is one of the most agriculturally fertile areas in Italy, with cereals and fodder predominant; there is also cattle farming and fruit production in the area.

Fiera Milano (the Great Milan Fair) is something of a misnomer since the trade fair centre hosts fairs for most of the year. With July, August and December the only quiet months, the busiest times are spring and autumn, from the fair on tourism in February to fashion in March, furniture in April, and technology, fashion and shoe fairs in September and October. (Milan's booming economy means that hotels may be hard to find during fairs.)

Pinnacle of banking

City layout

It is still possible to recognise the square core of the original Roman settlement at the Piazza di San Sepolcro. The oval plan of the medieval city is today marked by the broad inner ring road which runs from the Castello Sforzesco in the northwest round to the hospital district in the southeast. This encloses most of the city's sights. The fortifications built while the city was under Spanish rule in the 16th century mark the extent to which Milan had expanded by the end of the Middle Ages.

These fortifications now lie buried beneath the central ring of main roads (the so-called *convallazione interna, see map page 96*). After further growth due to industrialisation during the 19th century, which extended its borders to the canal ring *(Cerchia dei Navigli)* and the outermost ring road *(Circonvallazione esterna)*, the city is nowadays expanding primarily towards the north, where many of Italy's biggest companies have relocated, creating their own infrastructure in the process. IBM, for example, has settled in Segrate to the northwest of the city.

Likewise, to the south, clusters of satellite towns have sprung up – less the result of planning initiatives than of real estate speculation. They are still outside the public transport network, and are connected to the city centre by expressways.

Since the destruction inflicted by Allied bombing raids in World War II, the city has been substantially modernised. But, in the city centre, around the magnificent Cathedral, there are still a large number of classical buildings, and there's the sense of an older Milan – enhanced by an ongoing programme of restoration and renovation.

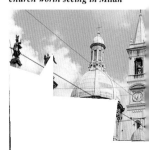

The Cathedral isn't the only church worth seeing in Milan

Historical Highlights

396BC The original settlement founded by the Umbrian Etruscans in the 6th century BC is over-run in an attack by the Celtic tribe of the Insubres. In the 3rd century BC the latter pitch themselves against a Rome that is becoming ever stronger.

222BC The town of the Insubres is conquered by Roman consul Marcus Claudius Marcellus. From Mediolanum (Milan) Roman culture spreads across the province of Gallia Cisalpina (Cisalpine Gaul), which covers the whole of Northern Italy.

49BC The inhabitants of Gallia Cisalpina are granted Roman civic rights. With the emergence of the Empire, the importance of Milan grows steadily.

AD293 The Empire is reorganised under Diocletian, Milan becomes the residence of Co-emperor Maximian and capital of the Western Empire.

313 The 'Milan Edict of Tolerance': Emperor Constantine grants the Christians religious freedom.

374 The governor of Emilia-Liguria, Aurelius Ambrosius, is elected Bishop of Milan, despite not being baptised. He becomes one of four Fathers of the Church and has a strong influence on the political course of the state and the cultural development of Milan. In 387 he baptises the most influential Father of the Church, St Augustine of Hippo.

402 After the city is plundered by the Visigoths under Alaric I in 400, Emperor Honorius and his retinue leave Milan, which relinquishes its role as the capital of the Western Empire (from 404, the emperor resides in Ravenna).

452 Attila's Huns conquer the Po Basin and Milan; the city enters a period of decline.

476 The fall of the West Roman Empire. The Goths take over the reins of power: at first the mercenary leader Odoacer, then the Ostrogoth King Theodoric the Great, who destroys Milan in 539. In 553 the Ostrogoths succumb to the army of Byzantine Emperor Justinian.

568 Under King Alboin I the Lombards invade Northern Italy. In 569 most of Milan's population flees before the cruel attacks of the king, who makes Pavia his residence. Only in 584 do the Milanese return to their city, now in the hands of the milder King Authari and his Catholic-inclined spouse, Theodelinda of Bavaria. In Monza, their favourite residence, the queen founds the first Lombard Catholic church.

773–4 Charlemagne conquers the Lombard kingdom and absorbs it into his Frankish Empire. After the division of the Frankish Empire under his grandsons (843), Lombardy first falls to the central kingdom of Lothair I and then from 881–7 to the East Frankish kingdom of Charles III the Fat.

888–962 The impotence of the late Carolingians allows local princes to emerge, who come into conflict with one another. In 962, responding to a call for help from the Papal States, the German King Otto I conquers Northern Italy and is crowned by the pope. From now on the German kings see themselves as the rulers of the Lombard kingdom. At the end of the 10th century, the prosperous towns of Northern Italy cast aside the rule of the princes installed by the German kings. A struggle ensues between the Ghibellines (followers of the German emperor) and the Guelphs (supporters of the pope).

1018 Heribert of Intimiano becomes archbishop of Milan. He creates the economic base for the Milan Communes, and is instrumental in the coronation of Conrad II (crowned king of Italy at Pavia in 1026 and emperor in Rome one year later), who founds a new imperial dynasty.

1154–83 Emperor Frederick I Barbarossa tries unsuccessfully to subdue the Lombard cities, but Milan is destroyed in 1162. After the creation of the Lombard League (1167) under the leadership of Milan, the cities defeat the emperor in 1176 near Legnano. In the Peace of Constance (1183) the emperor is forced to recognise their independence.

1236 Emperor Frederick II leads a bitter struggle against the Lombard League, which he defeats in 1237 in the battle of Cortenuova. He imposes a rigid government on Northern Italy, but the Stauffen dynasty falls shortly after the death of the emperor.

1262 Ottone Visconti becomes archbishop of Milan. The Ghibelline nobility allies itself with the archbishop in the struggle against the Guelphs, led by the Torriani family. The internal power struggles finally end with the destruction of the free communes and lead to the installation of the Signoria, the 'rule of tyranny'.

1311 Matteo Visconti becomes uncontested ruler of Milan.

1395 Gian Galeazzo Visconti becomes duke of Milan, and during his Golden Age the Duchy's influence extends to Verona, Bologna and Genoa.

1447 After the death of Duke Filippo Maria Visconti the Aurea Republica Ambrosiana, a short-lived democracy, is established.

1450 The condottiere Francesco Sforza, the son-in-law of the last Visconti, becomes duke of Milan. Another Golden Age ensues, especially during the reign of Lodovico il Moro (1479–99).

1499 On account of his blood ties with the Viscontis, Louis XII of France claims the Duchy of Milan for himself and conquers the city. In 1512, the Sforza succeed in returning, but only briefly.

1525 Francis I of France, who is attempting to conquer Northern Italy and has rid Milan of the Sforzas, is defeated near Pavia by Charles V.

1540 Charles V bequeaths the Duchy of Milan to his son, later Philip II of Spain. With the division of the Habsburg Empire in 1556, Milan falls to Spain, and remains under Spanish rule until 1714.

1560 Carlo Borromeo (canonised in 1610) becomes Archbishop of Milan, and embarks on far-reaching reforms within the Catholic Church.

1701–14 The War of the Spanish Succession: between Austria, Prussia, England, Holland and Portugal on one side, and Louis XIV allied with Bavaria on the other. At the end of the war, the Duchy of Milan falls to Austria, which maintains its rule over the city with only short interruptions until 1859.

1796 During the Wars of the Coalitions, Napoleon Bonaparte conquers Lombardy. In 1797 he creates Cisalpine Republic, with Milan as capital.

1802 Napoleon makes himself president of the Italian Republic that has emerged from the Cisalpine Republic. In 1805 he is crowned king of Italy in Milan.

1814–15 After the fall of Napoleon, the Congress of Vienna reaffirms Austria's claims to Lombardy.

1848 With the support of the Sardinian Royal House, the House of Savoy, the leaders of the Italian Unity Movement (Risorgimento) oust the Austrians from Milan; however, they win it back at the Battle of Custoza on 6 August.

1859 Austria declares war on Sardinia, which is allied with Napoleon II. After defeats at Magenta and Solferino, Austria hands Lombardy to Sardinia.

1861 Victor Emanuel II becomes king of Italy. Rome becomes the capital of the new kingdom.

1900 King Umberto I is murdered in Monza.

1922 From Milan Benito Mussolini begins his March on Rome with his Fascist black-shirts.

1939 Mussolini signs the Pact of Steel with Hitler.

1945 On 27 April, while fleeing to Switzerland, Mussolini is shot at Tremezzo on Lake Como.

1946 Italy becomes a republic.

1963 The Archbishop of Milan, Cardinal Montini, is elected Pope Paul VI (dies 1977).

1972 Giulio Andreotti forms his first government.

1992 A Milan businessman refuses to pay a bribe to a local politician. Di Pietro, a Milan magistrate, dares to investigate, and the corrupt post-war order of Italian politics collapses.

1994 National elections usher in a new Italian Republic, an electoral system modelled along British 'first-past-the-post' lines.

1996 Italy run by its first centre-left government. Romano Prodi is the new Premier. He resigns in 1998 after a vote of no confidence.

1997 Fashion giant Gianni Versace is murdered. Playwright Dario Fo, born in Parabiago in the Milan Province, wins the Nobel Prize for Literature.

1998 The revamped and expanded Malpensa airport opens.

1999 Italy adopts the euro currency.

Route 1

Milan Cathedral

Open daily 6.45am–7pm. Note that you will not be allowed into the Cathedral if you are wearing shorts, a short skirt or if your shoulders are uncovered.

Any thoughts of Milan are inextricably linked with this masterpiece of Italian Gothic, and indeed the gigantic ★★★ **Cathedral** (the Duomo) is the most important building in the city and Milan's greatest attraction.

A Gothic masterpiece

12

The main facade

Even if stylistically speaking the Cathedral is not as pure as some of its counterparts in France – a fact that can be explained by the length of time it took to build – the building impresses because of its massive dimensions and elegant proportions. Milan Cathedral is the best example of Gothic architecture in Italy. But it also demonstrates more clearly than any other building the conflict between the vernacular Lombard style and the northern Gothic, for the supervision of its construction lay not only with Lombard architects: on the exterior, the northern Gothic is evident in the flying buttresses and the upward-striving forms so typical of a French cathedral, while the Italian Gothic is manifested in the vast width of the edifice.

Work on the Cathedral began in 1386 at the instigation of Gian Galeazzo Visconti. It is not known who drew up the plans, and it is presumed that they were the combined effort of several Lombard master builders who had learned their trade working on the cathedral in Cologne. In the early years the supervision of the building lay in the hands of Italian, French and German masters, who replaced one another in rapid succession. The names include Simone da Orsenigo, Marco Frisone da Campione, Nicolas de Bonaventura from Paris, Giovannino and Salomone de Grassi from Como, Hans von Fernach, Ulrich von Ensingen (the builder of the cathedral spire in Strasbourg), Heinrich Parler (the designer of Ulm Cathedral), the Fleming Conrad Bruges and the Parisian Jean Mignot. The arguments between the foreign and local masters ended in 1400 with the appointment of Filippino degli Organi as supervisor, and in 1418 the high altar was ready to be consecrated by Pope Martin V. Towards the end of the 15th century, building was supervised by Guiniforte Solari and Giovanni Antonio Amadeo, two architects influenced by the Renaissance. In 1499 work was interrupted for a while upon the death of Lodovico il Moro; and after Amadeo passed away in 1522, progress came to a standstill.

It was only during the time of Cardinal Carlo Borromeo that work on the Cathedral was resumed. In 1567 Pellegrino Tibaldi was entrusted with continuing the project and drew up designs, according to the tastes of the time, for a magnificent baroque facade which stood in complete contrast to the rest of the building. In 1572 Carlo Borromeo consecrated the church to the memory of the birth of the Virgin Mary. Work on Tibaldi's facade was begun in 1616, but it was later transformed into Gothic style and remained incomplete. Work on the exterior continued during the 18th and 19th century: between 1805–13 Napoleon I had the west facade completed according to the plans of Carlo Amati, a period that also saw the completion of the decorative elements. Additions to the upper parts of the building date from the early 20th century and further work on the portals was carried out between 1948 and 1950.

Vital statistics
Santa Maria Nascente Cathedral is a five-naved basilica in the French idiom, with a triple-naved transept. The church has a length of 158m (520ft) and a width of 66m (215ft). With a length of 92m (300ft), the transept protrudes only a little from the line of the outer aisles. The central nave is 17m (55ft) wide and 48m (157ft) high. The interior height of the cupola is 68m (220ft) and the top of the crossing tower with the 4-m (14-ft) crowning statue of the Madonnina is 108m (355ft) above the ground. The main facade is 61m (200ft) wide and 56m (180ft) high. It is said that the Cathedral can house up to 40,000 people.

The exterior
The building is faced in white marble (from quarries north of Lago Maggiore). Some 135 tracery elements, as well as 2,245 statues and 96 atlases for supporting the gargoyles decorate the roof and exterior surfaces.

Delicate spires

13

Main facade
The facade is the least harmonious part of the building, because it reflects the variety of styles that succeeded each other during the course of its long period of construction. In particular, the lower half, with the classical-baroque elements by Pellegrino Tibaldi (16th century), stands in complete contrast to the Gothic forms of Carlo Buzzi on the upper half of the structure, something that is very evident in the differing shapes of the windows.

The plinths of the six massive vertical buttresses that divide the facade into five sections are decorated with reliefs depicting biblical stories, as well as supporting figures (17th–18th century). On the pillar consoles there are statues of the Apostles and Prophets (19th century).

Biblical reliefs

The early baroque portal surrounds are by Tibaldi, while the bronze doors date from the 20th century. With the exception of the central doorway, the designs embellishing them are all of Milanese motifs (*see Plan, page 14*):

A *The 'Milan Edict of Tolerance' of Constantine* (1948, by Arrigo Minerbi).

B *Scenes from the Life of St Ambrose* (1950, by Giannino Castiglioni).

C Portrayal of the *Family Tree and the Life of the Virgin Mary* (1894–1908, by Ludovico Pogliaghi).

D The history of Milan from its destruction at the hands of Frederick Barbarossa up to the victory at Legnano (1950, by F Lombardi and V Pessina).

E The history of the Cathedral up to the time of Carlo Borromeo (1950, by Luciano Minguzzi).

Milanese motifs on the bronze doors

The nave and the choir

Perhaps the best view of the Cathedral is the one from the Piazzetta Reale, to the southeast of the building, which reveals the whole length of the Duomo in all its glory, the walls of the nave broken by pillars and high windows, supported by powerful arched buttresses and surmounted by delicate tall pinnacles. The oldest part of the church is the apse (14th century) and between the 15th and 18th century the nave was gradually extended westwards towards the facade, the most recent part of the building. The magnificent tower above the crossing (16th century) is by Amadeo; between 1765–9 the main spire was added and subsequently crowned with the golden statue of the ★ *Madonnina* (1774, the Virgin and beloved city protector).

The Madonnina

14

The apse

Built in pre-Gothic style, the apse is not only the oldest but also the most beautiful part of the Cathedral. The three massive lancet windows (c 1390 by Nicolas de Bonaventura) are the largest in the world; their fine tracery is the work of Filippino degli Organi.

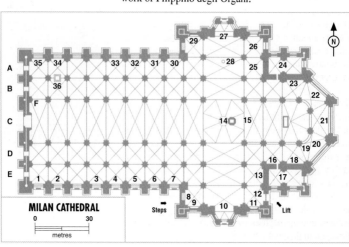

MILAN CATHEDRAL

0   30
metres

Steps   Lift

The terraces

The Cathedral's broad roof ★ ★ terraces are faced with marble slabs. These slabs lead all the way round the building and provide excellent views over the city and across as far as the outlying mountains, as well as a chance of examining some of the details such as the wonderful flying buttresses, gables, pinnacles, spires and statues more closely.

The terraces can be reached by taking a lift at the north-east side of the cathedral. The entrance is on the outside (March to October 9am–5.30pm, November to February 9am–4.30pm; entrance fee). There are quite a few steps to climb at the top of the lift, so it's advisable to wear stable flat shoes. This also helps you to feel more stable crossing the sloping roof.

The 14th-century *Guglia Carelli*, the Cathedral's oldest gable, is worthy of special attention; it is above the corner pilaster of the northern sacristy, facing the Corso Vittorio Emanuele and is named after its donor Marco Carelli. As far as statuary is concerned, *Eve* (16th century, the Solari school), to the south of the apse, and *Adam*, on its northern side, are worth a look.

Flying buttresses viewed from the terraces

The interior

The imposing main nave with its rows of double aisles either side is crossed by the transept with single aisles. The 52 composite pillars with their richly decorated capitals bear figures of the saints (mostly 1410–50, by Filippino da Modena). The interior contains 914 statues. The marble mosaic floor was designed by Tibaldi.

Immediately to the right of the entrance is the **Battistero di S Giovanni alle Fonti** [F], the baptistry in which St Augustine was baptised by St Ambrose on 24 April 387. It is open to the public from 9.30am–5.15pm.

Inside the Cathedral

1 Tomb of Archbishop Ariberto of Intimiano (1018–45); above, a copy of a priceless Lombard copper crucifix (11th century) that is now in the Museo del Duomo, and to the left a memorial tablet recalling the year the Cathedral was founded (1386).

2 Sarcophagus of Archbishop Ottone Visconti (died 1295) from the 14th century. Above and to the left of the tomb are two stained-glass windows portraying episodes from the Old Testament (15th century, by Nicolò da Varallo).

3 Sarcophagus of Marco Carelli (1408, by Filippino degli Organi). Above is another piece of stained glass by Nicolò da Varallo with more Old Testament scenes (15th century).

4 Tomb of Canon Gian Andrea Vimercati (died 1548), by Bambaia. To the right is a tablet with a design for a new cathedral facade (1886, by Brentano). The window above (1424, by Stefano da Pandino) has scenes from the New Testament.

5 Altar by Pellegrino Tibaldi (16th century) with the painting *Peter's visit to St Agatha* (1597, by Federico Zuccari). The window above depicts the life of St John the Evangelist.

6 Another altar by Tibaldi. Above, stained-glass window made in 1988, which depicts and is dedicated to Cardinals Schuster and Ferrari.

7 On the altar (also by Tibaldi) the marble sculpture *Madonna between St Catherine of Alexandria and St Paul* (1396).

8 Tomb of Gian Giacomo Medici, called *Medeghino* (died 1555), a general who served under Emperor Charles V. This masterpiece by Leone Leoni (1563) includes a statue of the Medici in Roman armour, surrounded by allegorical figures depicting bravery (left) and peace (right) as well as wisdom (left) and fame. Allegorical bronze reliefs depict the rivers Adda (left) and Ticino (right).

9 Altar donated by Pope Pius IV (16th century) at which Carlo Borromeo usually celebrated Mass. The window above (1564, by Corrado de Mochis) portrays *Scenes from the Life of St James*.

10 Cappella di San Giovanni Bono (17th century) built in memory of this 7th-century Milan bishop, whose life is depicted on the stained glass of the chapel.

11 Stained glass (1556, by Biagio and Giuseppe Arcimboldi) with *Scenes from the Life of St Catherine of Alexandria*. Underneath are two small doors to an underground passage leading directly to the archbishop's palace.

12 Altar with the marble portrayal of the *Presentation of Mary in the Temple* (1543, from the workshop of

Capella di San Giovanni Bono

Scenes from the life of St Catherine

Bambaia), as well as two reliefs on the column plinths depicting the *Birth and Marriage of Mary* (16th century, by Cristoforo Lombardo). The stained-glass window above depicts the life of *St Martin of Tours* (16th century).

13 To the right of the Altar of St Agnes is the gruesome statue of *St Bartholomew being Flayed Alive* (1562) bearing the boastful inscription 'It wasn't Praxiteles, but Marco d'Agrate that made me'.

14 The octagonal cupola over the crossing (68m/223ft) is embellished in its galleries with the figures of 60 saints (second half of the 15th century) and in the spandrels with the busts of the Fathers of the Church (1501, by Cristoforo Solari). In the centre of the crossing there is a bronze grill beneath which is the tomb of St Carlo Borromeo.

15 Choir. At the entrance pillars are two vast pulpits of gilded bronze and beaten copper (1590, by Pelizzoni) with biblical portrayals decorating the parapets. Then comes the Choir of Senators *(Coro Senatorio)* with the mighty organ from the 16th century, and beyond the *Santuario* with three rows of choir stalls (1572–1620) built according to the plans of Tibaldi; the inlays with scenes from the life of St Ambrose are by Paolo di Gazli. Stored in a niche in the vault way up above the choir is the Holy Nail of the Cross, a relic that is believed to have come from Christ's cross. Each year, on September 14, the Bishop of Milan is hoisted up to the niche on pulleys, so that he can show the nail to the public below.

The nave

Votive candles

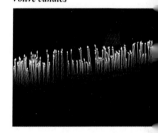

The centre of the sanctuary is taken up by the High Altar, another Tibaldi creation, which surrounds the original altar that was consecrated by Pope Martin V in 1418. The gilded ciborium above (1590, by Pelizzoni) embraces a tabernacle (1561, by Solari) which is protected by four angels and has reliefs showing scenes from the life of Christ and statues of Jesus and the disciples. Behind a copper copestone in the vault (with the image of God the Father, by Jacopino da Tradate) is kept the reliquary of *St Nagel* which is said to have been found by St Ambrose (put on display on 3 May).

The choir is lined with marble panels, which date from the early baroque period (after designs by Tibaldi). Two doors at the side of the choir lead to the crypt (1579, by Tibaldi, and richly decorated in the 17th century). From here one walks down into the octagonal **Funeral Chamber** (Scurolo, 1606, by Richini) of St Carlo Borromeo with its ceiling reliefs by Andrea Biffi. The saint rests in a coffin of rock crystal, which was a gift from Philip IV of Spain (9am–noon, 2.30–6pm).

Cathedral Treasures

Chrismon Sant' Ambrosii

16 Crypt. Steps opposite the sacristy lead down under the altar to the crypt, home to the Duomo's Treasury.

17 Southern sacristy (no access for visitors). The portal was constructed by the German Hans von Fernach, assisted by Porrino and Giovannino de Grassi.

Note that sections 18–23 are currently undergoing restoration and are hence inaccessible to visitors.

18 On a Gothic console is the statue of Pope Martin V (1424, by Jacopino da Tradate). Immediately to the left is the tomb of Cardinal Marino Caracciolo (16th century, by Bambaia).

19 Old marble panel (pre-11th century) called *Chrismon Sant' Ambrosii*, with engraved symbols of the Beginning and the End, the circle (symbol of God) and eight rays (symbol of eternal bliss).

20 Relief *Pietà between two Angels*, a German work dating from 1389.

21 Commemorative plaque to the consecration of the Cathedral on 20 September 1572 by Cardinal Carlo Borromeo.

22 Byzantine crucifix wrapped in stole and chasuble (13th century). The stained glass of the three large apse windows portrays events from the Old and New Testaments as well as scenes from the Apocalypse (mostly 19th century).

23 Seated statue of Pope Pius IV (1567, by Angelo de Marinis). The frescoes *A Crucified Man between Mary and the Saints* (probably by Isacco da Imbonate) and *Madonna with Child and John the Baptist* are both works of the early 15th century.

24 Northern Sacristy. The portal (14th century) is by Giacomo da Campione. The Angel of the ceiling frescos

(1611) was executed by Camillo Procaccini and the floor (15th century) was laid by Marco da Carona.

25 Baroque altar with marble altarpiece *St Hekla with the Lions* (1754, by Carlo Beretta).

26 Altar with marble altarpiece *Crucifix and Saints* (1594, by Marcantonio Prestinari). The stained-glass pictures above show scenes from the *Life of St John of Damascus* (1479, by Nicolò da Varallo).

To the left of the altar is the door to the *Scala dei Principi* (Counts' Staircase), used by notables to get on to the roof terraces. Above the door the modern piece of stained glass (by Beltrami) details the life of Carlo Borromeo.

27 Capella della Madonna dell'Albero. The baroque chapel of the 'Madonna of the Tree' (by Francesco Richini) contains the altarpiece *Virgin and Child* (1768, by Elia V Buzzi).

28 Celebrated Trivulzio candelabro. This seven-armed, 5-m (16-ft) high bronze candelabrum is a magnificent example of French art of the late 12th century and is thought to be the work of the goldsmith Nicolas de Verdun; in 1562 it was donated to the Cathedral by the priest Giambattista Trivulzio.

The Trivulzio Candelabro

19

29 The Gothic Altar of St Catherine (14th century) with statuary by Cristoforo Solari (15th century). The stained-glass windows above (16th century, by Corrado de Mochis) recount the story of *St Catherine of Siena*. The window to the left (1567, by Carlo Urbini) has scenes from the Acts of the Apostles.

30 Above a baroque altar by Tibaldi is the altarpiece *Ambrose Forces Emperor Theodosius to do Penance* (17th century, by Baroccio).

31 Altar by Tibaldi with a *Marriage of Mary* (16th century, by Frederico Zuccari). The window above deals with scenes from the lives of the Evangelists.

32 Cappella del Crofisso (Chapel of the Crucifix). A further Tibaldi altar with the wooden crucifix that Carlo Borromeo proceeded through Milan during the plague of 1562. The stained glass above (16th century, by Valerio Profundavalle) portrays *Scenes from the Lives of the Evangelists*.

33 Replica of the tomb of General Alessio Tarchetta (original fragments in the Castello Sforzesco). The stained glass above (1565–66, by Corrado de Mochis and Pier Angelo Sessini) depicts the life of the Virgin Mary.

34 Two tablets of red Veronese marble bearing relief figures of eight Apostles.

35 A sundial on the wall with the sign of the Capricorn. Its light comes from an opening opposite.

36 Baptistry (16th century, by Tibaldi) in the shape of a small temple. The font is a Roman urn made of porphyry, dating from the 2nd–3rd century AD.

Piazza del Duomo

Palazzo Settentrionale

Route 2

Piazza del Duomo – Palazzo Reale – Piazza Mercanti – Galleria Vittorio Emanuele – Teatro alla Scala – Museo Poldi-Pezzoli

The heart of Milan is the **Piazza del Duomo** (Cathedral Square). Even in the Middle Ages this is where the religious life of the city was focused, while the administrative centre was concentrated barely 100m (328ft) to the west around the Piazza dei Mercanti. Back in Roman times the centre of the town, the Forum, was located to the southwest on the site of the present-day Piazza San Sepulcro.

The Cathedral Square was given its present appearance between 1862 and 1878 by the architect Giuseppe Mengoni: along the long sides of the once modest square he constructed the two blocks of buildings with colonnades, the Palazzo Meridionale in the south and the Palazzo Settentrionale in the north with the imposing entrance to the Galleria Vittorio Emanuele (*see page 25*). Opposite the cathedral, the square is completed by the Palazzo dell'Orologio.

In the middle of the Cathedral Square stands the **monument to Victor Emanuel II** (1896, by Ercole Rosa). The bronze equestrian statue shows the king at the battle of San Martino (1859); the reliefs on the plinth depict the entry of French-Piedmontese troops into Milan after the battle of Magenta (1859).

Palazzo Reale

Immediately to the southeast of the Cathedral Square is the little Piazzetta Reale, with the **Palazzo Reale ❶**. In the 11th and 12th century this was the site of the Broletto Vecchio, Milan's old town hall, which became the residence of the Viscontis in 1310. Between 1330 and 1336 Azzone Visconti had the building converted into the magnificent Corte Ducale Viscontea (Ducal Court of the Viscontis). The building lost its importance when the front part of the palace was removed to make way for the Cathedral, and when in 1385 the Viscontis moved into the Castello Sforzesco (*see page 42*). Between the 16th and 17th centuries, when the remainder of the building became the residence of the Spanish governor, the former courtyard, today's Piazzetta Reale, served as the ceremonial entrance. In the 18th century this was the location of Milan's very first opera house.

Victor Emanuel II statue

The palace was given its present neoclassical countenance between 1771 and 1778 when it became the residence of the Austrian Archduke Ferdinand; the radical alterations were carried out under the direction of Giuseppe Piermarini. After the unification of Italy (1861), the building was named the Royal Palace. Umberto I often used to stay here.

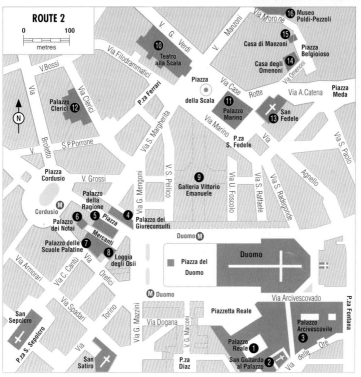

On the second floor of the Palazzo Reale, the collection of the **Civico Museo d'Arte Contemporanea (CIMAC)** provides a superb summary of the works of European artists of the 19th and 20th centuries. It consists partly of works that were obtained during the course of the 20th century and partly of paintings donated by the collectors Ausonio Canavese (including works by the Futurist, Umberto Boccioni) and Antonio Boschi, as well as from the artists Fontana and Melotti. Apart from them, emphasis is given to the Futurists and abstract artists, with works by Gino Rossi, Modigliani, Savinio, de Chirico, Severini, and Morandi, as well as the *Corrente* artists and the Lombard *Chiarismo*. Moreover there is the exhibition of the precious Jucker Collection.

The galleries are open from 9.30am– 5.30pm; closed Monday; tel: 02-62083219. Admission free.

A side wing (Piazza Duomo 14) houses the **Museo del Duomo** (9.30am–12.30pm and 3–6pm; closed Monday, except when this is a national holiday, Easter, 1 May, 15 August, Christmas; admission free). The following is a list of the various rooms in the museum, including details of their main exhibits:

Plaque of the Museo del Duomo

The Deposition

Warrior in Armour

*Da Varallo's Creation
of the Animals*

I	(Entrance hall.) Photography of the Cathedral as well as marble plaques with the trademark of the 'Honourable Cathedral Construction Site' (explanations only in Italian).
II	In the middle stands *St Agnes* (1491, by Benedetto Briosco); to the right are three marble statuettes from the 14th century that previously stood on the Carelli-Fiale; the original cast of the *Madonnina*, (the Virgin, 1769, by Perego); a number of Flemish works, including the *Deposition* (16th century); reproductions of drawings of the Cathedral's construction, including works by Leonardo da Vinci.
III	In the middle stands *St George* (1404, by Georgio Solari, which displays the facial features of Gian Galeazzo Visconti); various mouldings of gargoyles (15th century); *Warrior in Armour* (1404, by Matteo Raverti); *Titan* (15th century, German school).
IV	Plaster-cast of the monument to Pope Martin V. In the middle is *St Paul the Hermit* (c 1470, by Cristoforo Mantegazza).
VI	Terracotta studies from the 17th and 18th century; *St Sebastian* (15th century); two Flemish Gobelin tapestries (16th century) depicting scenes from the Old Testament. In the middle of the hall is *Jonah* (15th century, by Cristoforo Solari) and *Joshua* (late 15th century).
VII	On the entrance corbels are *Jesus* and *Mary* (15th century); on the walls, terracotta studies for the facade reliefs (17th century) and, above them, the matching distemper paintings by G B Crespi; in the middle of the room is *St Sebastian* (15th century, Lombard); *St Agapitus at the Stake* (1607, by Andrea Biffi); *Disputation of the Doctors of the Church* (late 16th century, an early work by Tintoretto).
VIII/IX	Further exhibits from the 15th–17th century.
X	A wooden model of the Cathedral (c 1520) stands in the centre; other models of various facade designs including the one by Giuseppe Brentano from 1888, which was awarded first prize in an international competition but was never realised.
XI	In the middle is a bronze model of the main spire of the Cathedral; more designs for the facade can also be seen.
XII	Pieces of marble from the quarries of Candoglia, which from 1386 provided the building material for the Cathedral; also here are mouldings of portal reliefs.

The Palazzo Reale complex also contains the former ducal chapel of **San Gottardo al Palazzo** ❷ (entrance in Via Pecorari, Monday to Friday 8am–noon and 2–6pm, Saturday 8am–4pm, Sunday 8am–1pm). It was built in 1336 by Francesco Pecorari and, just like the Palazzo Reale, was redone in 1770 in the neoclassical style by Piermarini. From the Gothic era remain the entrance portal and the elegant octagonal bell tower, which is crowned with the gilded statue of St Michael. The warm brick tones of the tower form a particularly stunning contrast to the white of the little columns at its top. The interesting apse which has gable windows and a dwarf gallery dates from the 14th century and is from an even earlier building.

San Gottardo al Palazzo

Inside, to the left of the high altar, is the barely intact tomb of the donor of the church, Azzone Visconti, a work by Giovanni di Balduccio (14th century); the fresco opposite (17th century, by Cerano) is of St Carlo Borromeo. On the rear wall of the nave a fragment of the fresco *Crucifixion* (Giotto school) has been preserved.

The next place to visit on this route is the **Palazzo Arcivescovile** ❸, the Archbishop's Palace. First built in 1170, it was transformed and extended several times during the following centuries, particularly during the tenure of Cardinal Carlo Borromeo by the architect Pellegrino Tibaldi (16th century). The facade facing eastwards to the Piazza Fontana (1784–1801) was the work of Piermarini, who was also responsible for the large fountain in the middle of the square (from here there is a great view of the cathedral spire). The doorway in the facade leads through to a cloister (15th–17th century) which gives access to the Palace Chapel (18th century, by Piermarini) and some living quarters (closed to the public).

Palazzo Arcivescovile

23

Cool corner

In Via Arcivescovado, on the north side of the palace, are the remains of medieval structures and Gothic brick windows (14th century). Now go through the large marble doorway by Tibaldi (house No 6); it leads to the second of the palace's courtyards, the *Cortile della Canonica* (Canons' Courtyard), which was also built according to the designs of Tibaldi, and contains the massive statues of *Moses* (1865, by Tantardini) and *Aaron* (1864, by Strazzo).

On the other side of the Piazza Duomo is a delightful corner of medieval Milan, the ★ **Piazza Mercanti**. This was the centre of city life during the time of the free communes. The Piazza formed a closed square, from which six gates led out into the six districts that then comprised the town. In order to facilitate traffic, in 1865 the Via Mercanti was extended through the square, thus robbing it of its closed character. But the Piazza Mercanti is still a peaceful place, despite ongoing renovation, with a beautiful fountain in the middle (16th century), and surrounded by a number of notable buildings (4–8).

The **Palazzo dei Giureconsulti** ➍ was built in 1562 by Vincenzo Seregni by order of Pope Pius IV (Angelo Maria Medici), who originally hailed from Milan. The building, the upper storey of which was only completed in the 17th century, was the seat of the College of Jurists – the body that trained new recruits for the higher municipal offices. The richly decorated windows on the upper floor are adorned with the busts and coats-of-arms of the House of Medici. The building also includes the Torre di Napo, a tower erected in 1272 by Napo Torriani, whose bell was tolled at the times of execution. A statue of St Ambrose is contained in a niche beneath the tower's clock (1833, by Scorzini). Today the building is the home of the chamber of commerce (tel: 02-85151 to see inside).

Palazzo della Ragione

The ★ **Palazzo della Ragione** ➎ was once the home of the council chambers and law courts and is now used for exhibitions. It was built between 1228 and 1233 under the auspices of the mayor Oldrado da Tresseno, and remains the most important building from the time of the Milan commune. The lower floor of the Romanesque building consists of a triple-aisled, columned hall in which public assemblies were held; later this became the meeting place for bankers. With its triple-arched windows, the upper floor was originally crowned with three parapets. In 1770 during the reign of Maria Theresa it was converted to house the notarial archives, though it no longer performs this function today. Above the fourth column from the left is a distinctive Late Romanesque relief depicting the mayor Oldrado da Tresseno on horseback (1223, by Benedetto Antelami). The inscription underneath pays tribute to his services as the builder of the palazzo and as an enemy of heretics.

Oldrado da Tresseno

Above the second arch on the left is the former entrance to the council chamber, which was approached from an external staircase. Today access is through the connecting building on the west side of the square. It consists of just one room 50m (160ft) by 18m (60ft), which still bears traces of the original frescoes.

The legal archive was once housed in the **Palazzo dei Notai** ➏. Features of the original Late-Gothic building (15th century) that are still preserved are the pointed-arch loggia and one lancet window with richly ornamented brick surround.

Palazzo dei Notai

Based on the design for the Palazzo dei Giureconsulti, the **Palazzo delle Scuole Palatine** ➐ was erected in 1645 by Carlo Buzzi on the site of the former school building of the College of Jurists, which had been destroyed by fire. With the exception of the facade, the palazzo was rebuilt in the 19th century. The name recalls the officials' school of the Roman emperor. Next to the second window from the left is a statue of St Augustine, who was a teacher of

Rhetoric in Milan. Above the doorway to the Via Orefici is the statue of the Roman poet Ausonius (310–95), who once praised Milan in his verses.

The **Loggia degli Osii**  was built in 1316 by Matteo Visconti to replace the houses of the Osii family, and was used for the pronouncement of judgements and laws. The building was given its present appearance through restoration work carried out in 1904. The arches of the ground floor support a frieze with the coats-of-arms of Milan's districts and the Viscontis. Above the pointed arch on the upper floor the triple-arched windows have been partly converted into niches. These house the statues of the Virgin, the Infant Jesus and the seven patron saints of Milan (14th century, possibly by Jacopo da Tradate).

After this journey into medieval Milan it is a good idea to stroll along the north side of the Cathedral Square and enter the glorious ★ ★ **Galleria Vittorio Emanuele** ❾.

Galleria Vittorio Emanuele

This monumental complex of intersecting arcades forms the link between the Piazza del Duomo and the Piazza della Scala. It is often referred to as the Salon of Milan, because, with its elegant cafés and shops, it is the place where people traditionally converge. Built between 1865 and 1867 according to the plans of Giuseppe Mengoni, in Renaissance style, the Galleria was one of the earliest buildings to use cast iron and glass in its construction. In 1878, a 38.5-m (125-ft) high triumphal arch facing the Cathedral was added. The arcades are 197m (645ft) and 105m (345ft) long respectively and have a width of 14.5m (47ft) and height of 26m (85ft). In the middle of the gallery they form a 47-m (154-ft) high octagon with a glass dome measuring 39m (127ft) in diameter. The mosaics of the lunettes represent the continents. The triumphal arch of the gallery is draped with painted panels, which recall a stage set.

The octagonal dome

At the end of the gallery is the Piazza della Scala (currently undergoing restoration), in the middle of which is a **monument to Leonardo da Vinci** and his Milanese students Boltraffio, Salaino, Marco d' Oggiono and Cesare da Sesto (1872, by Pietro Magni). The reliefs portray the different fields of work in which Leonardo was involved: painting (*Last Supper*), anatomy (equestrian statue of Sforza), architecture (fortifications) and physics (hydraulic engineering).

Detail on the da Vinci monument

The northwest side of the square is occupied by the world-famous opera house ★★ **Teatro alla Scala** ❿. Although the exterior of the building is not especially imposing, the Teatro alla Scala, with its 2,000 seats, is still by far the largest theatre in Europe. The opening of the season on the day of the city's patron saint St Ambrose (7 December) is the greatest society event of the year, with opera, concerts and ballet (*see page 87*). 'La Scala', as the theatre is known for short, is famous for its marvellous

Pausing on the piazza

acoustics; to have an engagement here is the highest aim of performers from the world of opera.

Milan owes its opera house to Empress Maria Theresa who, after the old Teatro Regio Ducale burned down in 1776, approved the plan for a new theatre to be built 'at the expense of the people of Milan', but then actually covered most of the costs herself. Built in neoclassical style by Giuseppe Piermarini, the building stands on the site of the old Church of Santa Maria della Scala, which in 1385 had been donated by Regina della Scala, the wife of Bernabò Visconti – hence the name of the opera house. The ceremonial opening took place on 3 August 1778 with a performance of the opera *L'Europa riconosciuta* (Europe's Recognition), a work by the Vienna court composer Antonio Salieri – adversary of Mozart and teacher of Beethoven, Schubert and Liszt.

In 1812, the 12-year-old Gioacchino Rossini achieved his first sensational success here. In 1822, Gaetano Donizetti made his debut at La Scala, for which he wrote six operas. In 1829 came the première of Vincenzo Bellini's *Foreigner*, one of the greatest successes the opera house ever witnessed. These three composers dominated the scene until 1839, when the young Giuseppe Verdi came to La Scala with his mediocre work *Oberto Conte di San Bonifacio*. The Verdi era, in which the opera house reached unimaginable heights, had begun. Also the international success of Giacomo Puccini's *Madame Butterfly* started at La Scala.

After a short period of crisis, the arrival of Arturo Toscanini heralded an era in which the famous conductor transformed La Scala once again into one of the leading houses in the world. In 1943 the building was severely damaged by bombs, but as early as 11 May 1946 La Scala was reopened with a concert conducted by Toscanini.

Teatro alla Scala

The simple facade with its little portico is not very high; in the tympanum there is a flat relief, *Apollo's Sun Chariot* (1778). The auditorium was redesigned in 1807 by Giovanni Perego, and the renovation work necessary after World War II followed Perego's plans. The hall is 24m (78ft) long, 61m (200ft) wide and 26m (85ft) high. There are two rows of boxes and two galleries. A grand chandelier, designed by Sanquirico in 1830, hangs from the ceiling. The Scala can be visited except when rehearsals are in progress, from the Museo Teatrale (*see below*). The visit enables you to walk into the large mirror-lined upstairs foyer, which was overhauled in 1936, and from here you have access to several boxes, from which you may view the lush, deep-red and gold interior of the house. Photography is not allowed.

In the colonnade to the left of the opera house is the **Museo Teatrale alla Scala** (May to October daily 9am–12.30pm, 2–5.30pm, November to April closed on Sunday; entry up to 30 minutes before closing; tel: 02-8053418). The Theatre Museum was founded in 1913 and in addition to documenting the history of La Scala, it celebrates Greek and Roman theatre and Old Italian comedy. Of special interest are the two rooms of the Verdi collection, which provide a rich pictorial documentation of the life of the master, including some original scores. Liszt's piano, several death masks – including one of Wagner – and some fine portraits of Maria Callas are also notable.

Bust of Enrico Caruso

Opposite La Scala stands Milan's impressive town hall, the ★ **Palazzo Marino** ⓫. This boldly proportioned building was commissioned in 1558 to Galeazzo Alessi by the Genoese Tomaso Marino who had attained extraordinary wealth in Milan. Building work almost came to a standstill after the death of the artist in 1572; the palace changed hands several times before being taken over by the city in 1861. The facade facing the Piazza della Scala was erected between 1888 and 1890 by Luca Beltrami. The Palace contains a magnificently ornamented inner courtyard; on the ground floor the Alessi Hall, with its beautiful stucco and paintings, is also well worth seeing. Just like the Galleria, the Palazzo Marino is 'packed' in walls resembling a theatre set (visits by appointment only, tel: 02-62085118).

Palazzo Marino

Those with enough time on their hands can now progress westwards to the **Palazzo Clerici** ⓬. In addition to its other staterooms (Hall of Mirrors, Golden Hall), this early 18th-century palazzo contains the so-called Galleria degli Arazzi (Gobelin Gallery). On the richly decorated walls hang four priceless 17th-century Flemish tapestries. Especially valuable is the ceiling fresco executed by the Venetian baroque painter Giambattista Tiepolo c 1740: *Mercury Driving the Sun Chariot*. In this

San Fedele, with interior detail

Three of the caryatids

Doorway to Casa Manzoni

fresco, Mercury races across the heavens inhabited by Olympian gods, passing the people and animals symbolising the continents en route.

Those who decide not to take the above detour should proceed straight from the Piazza alla Scala along the Via Marino to the Piazza San Fedele, with its monument to the poet Alessandro Manzoni (1883, by Barzaghi). Beyond is the Jesuit church of **San Fedele** ⓭ (Monday to Friday 8.30am–2.30pm and 4–7pm). It was built between 1569 and 1579 by Pellegrino Tibaldi and is typical of Milanese 16th-century architecture. There are some beautiful paintings inside: to the right of the first altar is a *St Ignatius in Glory* (16th century, by Giovanni Battista Crespi, called Cerano) and to the right of the second altar a *Transfiguration* (1565, by Bernardino Campi), as well as, to the left of the first altar, a *Descent from the Cross* (16th century) by Simone Petersano, the tutor of Caravaggio. Alongside the carved confessionals (16th century, by Taurini) and the choir-stalls (16th century, by Anselmo del Conte) is the sacristy, which on account of its exquisitely carved cupboards is considered the most beautiful in Milan (the entrance is behind the second altar on the right).

Behind the Church of San Fedele begins the narrow Via Omenoni; it acquired its name from the eight large caryatids (by Antonio Abbondio) on the lower half of the facade of the **Casa degli Omenoni** ⓮. The celebrated sculptor Leone Leoni, called Aretino, built this house for himself in 1573. The frieze running under the cornice bears the relief *Lions Tear the Calumnition Apart*.

On the adjoining Piazza Belgioioso is the distinctive-looking palazzo of the same name (1772–81, by Piermarini) and on the left the **Casa di Manzoni** ⓯ (9am–noon and 2–4pm; closed on Monday, Saturday, Sunday and holidays; admission free). This was the residence of the poet Alessandro Manzoni from 1814 until his death on 22 May 1873. The study is situated on the ground floor. On the first floor are the dining-room, the drawing room (original furnishings from 1861, portraits of a number of Manzoni's friends including the great German man of letters, Goethe, with his signature), the bedroom (picture of the poet, 1847), and the room in which he died. The first editions of all Manzoni's works can be found in the gallery. Opposite is Boeucc, a Milanese culinary instituation (*see page 91*).

The route now follows Via Marone as far as the Via Manzoni with the ★★ **Museo Poldi-Pezzoli** ⓰, which is situated at house No 12 (Tuesday to Sunday, 10am–6pm; admission fee). Of all the private collections that were established in Milan during the 19th century, this one is probably the most notable. The museum was left as an art foundation in 1879 by the nobleman Gian Giacomo

Poldi Pezzoli. Alongside the paintings, the house of the collector contains a selected assortment of handicrafts, sculpture, textiles, weapons and instruments dating from Roman times onwards. The building was badly damaged during the war, but its 25 rooms were rebuilt almost exactly according to their original form and decoration.

Ground floor

1 **Armoury** containing more than 1,000 Italian, German, Spanish and Oriental pieces restored in the museum's workshop. Collecting armour was the primary passion of Poldi Pezzoli.
2 **Fresco and cloth rooms**: the highlight here is the magnificent Persian carpet dating from 1542–3 depicting a hunting scene. There are other fine carpets and tapestries in the collection.
3 **Lace Collection**: fine collection of Italian lace from the 16th to 20th centuries incorporating recent private donations. Among the items on display is an Italian bedcover dating from the 17th century that once belonged to Poldi Pezzoli.
4 **Library**: contains some 3,500 antique books from the 15th to 19th centuries including incunabula, as well as some fine illustrated manuscripts dating from the 7th and 8th centuries.

29

Museo Poldi-Pezzoli: staircase

5 **Staircase**: at the base of the beautiful open staircase stands a baroque fountain by Petiti; the staircase itself is embellished with early 18th-century landscape paintings by Magnasco. It leads to the upper floor, which contains a marvellous collection of paintings.

First floor

Portrait by Vincenzo Foppa

6 **Lombard Rooms**: contain paintings of the Lombard School from the 15th to 16th centuries, including *Madonna with Child* (16th century) by Vincenzo Foppa; *Nursing Mother and Flight into Egypt* (c 1500) by Andrea Solario; *Madonna with Christ Child Picking Flowers* (16th century) by Boltraffio; the reputed *Mystical Wedding of St Catherine* (c 1500), painted by Bernardino Luini; the wood-carving *Marriage of Mary* (16th century).

7 **Ceramics Room**: this originally rococo-style room contains terracotta, European and Oriental porcelain and majolica, largely based on the collection of Poldi Pezzoli. The majority of the pieces are European, from Meissen to Vienna and Doccia to Capodimonte.
8 **Black Room**: the name of this room derives from the original colour of the walls, lined with inlaid ebony but largely destroyed during the bombardment. However, the wooden door with bas reliefs showing the four seasons and day and night remains. Exhibits include the sculpture *Faith in God* by Lorenzo Bartolini; *St*

The Ceramics Room

16th-century goblet

Catherine of Alexandria by Bergognone and *Artemis* by Maestro di Griselda.

9 **Bedroom**: contains portraits of Giuseppe Molteni's family and a collection of beautiful Murano glass from the 15th to 19th centuries, mostly from the collection of Poldi Pezzoli.

10 **Dante Room**: this room is the most fascinating in the house and is one of the best examples of historicism and the neogothic style that charcterised the late 19th century. Windows are painted with scenes from Dante's *Divine Comedy*.

11 **Picture room**: works by Pietro Lorenzetti, Cosmè Tura, Crivelli, Vitale da Bologna and Venetian painters of the 17th century, like Guardi, Canaletto, Tiepolo and Rosalba Carriera.

12 **Jewels and other treasures**: rich collection of gold, enamel and bronze works, as well as porcelain.

13 **Sundials**: a fine collection of over 200 pieces from the 16th to 19th centuries.

14 **Golden Room** (the finest section): *Mary with Child* and *Bewailing of Christ* by Botticelli (the former considered poor); *St Nicola da Tolentino* by Piero della Francesca; *Portrait of a Young Woman* (c 1450) by Pollainolo; also paintings by Giovanni Bellini, Andrea Mantegna, Cosmè Tura and Vivarini.

15 **Visconti Venosta Room**: includes an extraordinary processional cross attributed to Raffaello Sanzio.

16 **Clocks Room**: 129 valuable clocks and timepieces dating from the 16th–19th centuries.

17 **Ghislandi Room**: portraits by Vittore Ghislandi, P Borroni and G Ceruti.

Route 3

Palazzo di Brera – Cimitero Monumentale – Giardini Pubblici

After the visit to the Museo Poldi-Pezzoli (*see page 28*) a brief stroll along Via Alessandro Manzoni, one of Milan's grandest shopping streets, is very rewarding. It connects the Piazza della Scala with the Piazza Cavour (*see page 41*) and is lined with beautiful patrician houses such as the Casa Greppi (house No 6) and the Casa Antona Traversi (house No 10), both built by Canonica in neoclassical style between 1829 and 1831.

The Via G Verdi leads to the Via Brera (Metro stations Montenapoleone, line 3, Cairoli, line 1, and Lanza, line 2) and house No 15, the **Palazzo Cusani** 🔟. Originally built

Fine glass

Bust on Casa Greppi

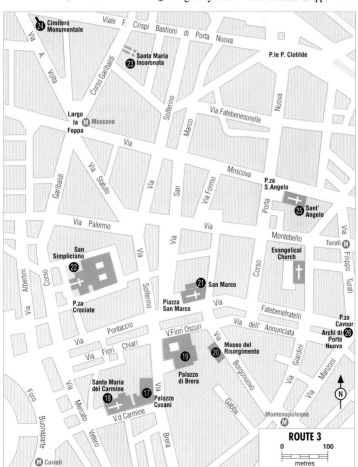

in the 17th century, the building was extended in 1719 by the architect Ruggeri in the style of the high baroque. The garden frontage, which can be seen from the Via del Carmine, is by Piermarini and represents a transitional style between baroque and neoclassicism.

Santa Maria del Carmine

A few steps further on is the church of **Santa Maria del Carmine** ⓱ (Monday to Friday 7.15–11.30am and 3.30–7pm, Saturday and Sunday till 7.30pm). This church, which belongs to the Carmelite monastery, was begun in 1339 according to the plans of Bernardo da Venezia, but then suddenly collapsed in 1446. It was subsequently rebuilt in Late-Gothic style under the direction of Pietro Solaris. After undergoing several major alterations down the centuries, the facade was converted into a Lombard Gothic fantasy style by Maciachini in 1879. Among the features particularly worth seeing on the inside is the splendid baroque chapel (1616–76) in the right transept, designed by Giovanni Quadrio (currently undergoing restoration). It was embellished with valuable, partly painted marble decorations by Procaccini. In the first chapel on the left there is a *Madonna with Child and Saints* (17th century) by Camillo Procaccini, while the fourth chapel on the left contains an early work by Bernardino Luini on the same theme (late 15th century). In the adjoining cloister there are fragments of Roman reliefs, medieval capitals and various sculptures by Campione masters.

The Palazzo di Brera

Back in Via Brera, the route soon leads to house No 28, the **Palazzo di Brera** ⓳. The present building, with its acclaimed art gallery the Pinacoteca di Brera, was erected for the Jesuit College according to the designs of F M Richini in 1651 on the site of a 12th-century monastery built outside the city for the Brothers of Mercy. After the abolition of the Jesuit Order in 1773, Maria Theresa founded here the Academy of Fine Arts whose collections formed the basis of the Pinacoteca. The magnificent main portal (1776–84) is by Piermarini. The rooms of the gallery had to be largely rebuilt after they were struck by bombs in 1943.

Alongside the art gallery, the palace today houses the **Biblioteca Braidense**, the largest library in the city, the Academy of Fine Arts, the Lombard Institute of Natural Sciences and Literature, as well as an observatory, where the **Astronomical Museum** is housed (Monday to Friday 9.30am–4.30pm, closed Saturday and Sunday; admission free). Here you can find astronomical aparatus which were used by the observatory for two centuries.

In front of the palace stands a monument to the painter Francesco Hayez (1890, by Barzaghi), who was once the director of the academy. The colonnades of the beautiful two-storey inner courtyard house the statues and busts of famous writers, artists and scholars. The middle of the courtyard is dominated by the bronze statue of *Napoleon as a Victorious Hero* (1809) by Antonio Canova. A monumental staircase leads up to the upper colonnade and the entrance to the ★★★ **Pinacoteca di Brera** (Tuesday to Friday, Sunday and public holidays 8.30am–7.15pm, Saturday 8.30am–11pm, last entry 35 minutes before closing; admission fee).

Napoleon in bronze

The foundations for this art collection, which is one of the most important in Italy, were laid at the end of the 18th and beginning of the 19th century. It was originally intended to be a didactic collection for the Art Academy. At the express wishes of Napoleon, his stepson Eugène Beauharnais had the art gallery opened to the public in 1809. With the oppression of various religious orders and their churches brought about by secularisation, numerous religious works of art were acquired by the state and added to the collection. During the course of the 19th and 20th century the collection has been considerably expanded through purchases and donations. It was further endowed with important works of contemporary art by the donations of the Jesi family. The Brera has around 2,500 works in its possession, principally by Italian masters of the 14th to 20th century, of which around 560 exhibits are on display in more than 30 rooms.

33

In 1976 there began a programme of renovation and re-organisation, intended to make the gallery conform to the changing needs of the present day (for example educational activities, changing exhibitions).

I
The hall contains the Jesi modern art collection, whose emphasis lies in Italian art from the first half of the 20th century. The collection includes works by Amedeo Modigliani, Umberto Boccioni, Carlo Carrà, Filippo de Pisis, Giorgio Morandi, Mario Sironi, Marino Marini and Medardo Rosso. There is also notable art from other European countries, including work by Pablo Picasso, Pierre Bonard and Georges Braque.

Sironi's 'Urban Landscape with Lorry' (1920)

IA
Reconstruction of the Chapel of Count Porro in Mocchirolo near Lentante, with the magnificent Gothic frescos (1365–70) by a Lombard master, possibly Pietra da Nova. The frecoes include: *Crucifixion, Christ and the Four Evangelists, Count Porro with Members of his Family Offering the Virgin a model of the Chapel, St Ambrose Enthroned Scourging Two Heretics*, and the *Mystic Marriage of St Catherine*. There is also a detached fresco by the less skilful Simone da Corbetta.

Chapel of Count Porro

Bellini's Pietà

St Mark by Master Giorgio

II–IV   Religious pictures from the 13th to 15th centuries, predominantly panel paintings and fragments of larger works that formed the altarpieces in the churches of the period. Painters represented include Giovanni Baronzio, Ambrogio Lorenzetti, Giovanni da Milano, Giovanni da Bologna, Nicolò di Pietro, Andrea di Bartolo, Stefano da Verona and Gentile da Fabriano.

V–VI   Venetian paintings of the 15th and 16th centuries, including, in Room V, the *Praglia Polyptych* by Giovanni d'Alemagna and Antonio Vivarini, *Dead Christ with Angels* by Girolamo da Treviso the Elder and *St Mark* by Master Giorgio; and, in Room VI, *Virgin and Child* (x2) by Giovanni Bellini, as well as his famous *Pietà* (see above), the eerily fore-shortened *Dead Christ* by Andrea Mantegna, and the *Marriage of the Virgin* and *Presentation of the Virgin* by Vittore Carpaccio.

VII   Venetian portraits of the 16th century. Lorenzo Lotto's *Portrait of an Elderly Gentleman with Gloves* and *Laura da Pola*, Titian's *Portrait of Count Antonio Porcia* and work by Tintoretto.

VIII   Venetian paintings of the 15th century. Works include the huge *St Mark Preaching in Alexandria* by Gentile and Giovanni Bellini, one of the Brera's most famous works; paintings by Bartolomeo Montagna including his *Virgin and*

Child Entroned with St Andrew, St Monica, St Ursula and St Sigismund, and Francesco Morone, Giovanni Mansueti, Alvise Vivarini and others.

IX Venetian paintings of the 16th century. This room is devoted to the greastest splendour of 16th-century Venetian painting and includes Titian's *St Jerome in Penitence*, Veronese's *Last Supper* and *Baptism and Temptation of Christ*, Tintoretto's *Finding of the Body of St Mark* and his *Pietà*, plus a *Pietà* by Lorenzo Lotto.

XIV Venetian paintings of the 16th century including Moretto da Brescia's *Virgin and Child* and Giovan Battista Moroni's *Virgin and Child with St Catherine, St Francis and Donor*.

Moroni's Virgin and Child with St Catherine, St Francis and Donor

XV Lombard paintings and frescoes of the 15th and 16th centuries, including Bramantino's *Virgin and Child and a Two Angels* and *Crucifixion*, and Vincenzo Foppa's Polyptych *Santa Maria delle Grazie*.

XVIII Lombard paintings of the 16th century, including Altobello Melone's *Portrait of Alda Gambara*, Callisto Piazza's *Baptism of Christ*, and a series of four paintings by Vincenzo Campi, considered to be the forerunners of the still life genre in Italy.

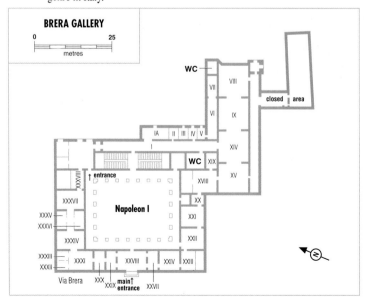

BRERA GALLERY

0   25
metres

WC

VII   VIII

closed | area

VI   IX

IA II III IV V

I

XIV

WC XIX

XXXIX ↑ entrance

XXXVII   XV

XVIII

Napoleon I   XX

XXXV   XXI

XXXVI

XXXIV   XXII

XXXIII XXXI XXVIII XXIV XXIII

XXXII

Via Brera   XXX   main ↑ entrance   XXVII
XXIX

Solario's Portrait of a Young Man

XIX Lombard religious paintings and portraits of the 15th and 16th centuries, including Bergognone's *Virgin and Child, St Catherine of Siena and a Carthusian Monk*, Andrea Solario's *Portrait of a Young Man* and *Virgin and Child with St Joseph and St Simeon*, and Bernardino Luini's *Madonna of the Rose Garden*.

XX 15th-century paintings from Ferrara and Emilia Romagna, including Francesco del Cossa's *St John the Baptist* and *St Peter*, Cosmè Tura's dramatic *Crucifixion*, and Lorenzo Costa's *Adoration of the Magi*.

XXI 15th-century polyptychs from the Marches, including *St Peter* by Fra Carnevale (Maestro delle Tavole Barberini), Girolamo di Giovanni's *Gualdo Tadino*, and Carlo Crivelli's *Coronation of the Virgin*.

XXII–III 15th- and 16th-century paintings from Ferrara and Emilia Romagna, including, in XXII, Marco Palmezzano's *Virgin and Child with Saints*, Lodovico Mazzolino's *Raising of Lazarus* and Dosso Dossi's *St Sebastian*; and, in XXIII, Corregio's *Nativity* and *Adoration of the Magi*.

Piero della Francesca's Urbino altarpiece

XXIV These rooms contain some of the finest works in the Brera, including *Madonna with Child, Angels, Saints and Federico da Montefeltro* by Piero della Francesca (altarpiece taken from the Church of S Bernardino in Urbino), *Marriage of the Virgin* by Raphael, *Christ at the Column* by Donato Bramante.

XXVII Central Italian Painting in the 15th and 16th centuries, including *Disputation over the Immaculate Conception* by Girolamo Genga and *The Virgin Annunciate with St John the Baptist and St Sebastian* by Timoteo Viti.

XXVIII Central Italian painting in the 17th century, including Ludovico Carracci's *Christ and the Samaritan Woman* and *The Sermon of St Anthony*, and Guido Reni's *St Peter and St Paul*.

Caravaggio's Supper at Emmaus

XXIX The works of Caravaggio (1570–1610) and pupils: *Supper at Emmaus* by Caravaggio, *Christ and the Samaritan Woman* by Battistello Caracciolo, and *The Martyrs Valerian, Tiburtius and Cecilia* by Orazio Gentileschi.

| XXX | Lombard painting in the 17th century, including *The Mystic Marriage of St Catherine* by Giulio Cesare Procaccini and *Virgin of the Rosary* by Cerano. |

Virgin and Child with St Anthony by Van Dyck

| XXXI | Flemish and Italian paintings of the 17th century, including works by Rubens, Van Dyck, Jacob Jordaens and Pietro da Cortona. |

| XXXII/ XXXIII | Flemish and Dutch paintings of the 16th and 17th centuries, including works by Jan de Beer, Rubens, Brueghel the Elder, and Van Dyck. |

| XXXIV | Religious painting of the 18th century, including works by Tiepolo, Subleyras and Bottani. |

| XXXV | 18th-century Venetian paintings, with works by Piazzetta, Canaletto (*The Bacino di San Marco from the Point of the Dogana*) and Bellotto. |

| XXXVI | Italian 18th-century genre painting and portraiture, including works by Crespi and Ceruti. |

37

| XXXVII–III | Italian 19th-century painting, including Francesco Hayez's sentimental work, *The Kiss*. Exit via Giuseppe Pelizza da Volpedo's *Fourth Estate*. |

After visiting the Palazzo di Brera, follow Via Fiori Oscuri to Via Borgonuovo and house No 23, the **Museo del Risorgimento** ⑳ (Tuesday to Sunday 9.30am–5.30pm; closed on Monday and public holidays; admission free).

The museum, which is housed in the Palazzo de Marchi (1775, by Piermarini), not only contains objects from the struggles of the Italian Unity Movement, but also memorabilia of Napoleon I (including the royal insignia and the robe he wore for his coronation as King of Italy) as well as exhibits from both world wars.

Now follow the Borgonuovo back to the north; at the end of it is the Church of **San Marco** ㉑ Monday to Saturday 7am–noon, 4–7pm, Sunday 7am–1pm). With a length of 96m (314ft), this is Milan's second largest church after the Cathedral. It is said that it was founded in 1254 by Lanfranco da Settala, who was later to become master of the Augustinian Order. Alterations were made in the 14th and again in the 17th century.

San Marco

After deconsecration of the patricians' cemetery that had been added to the church in the 15th century, between the 16th and 19th century nine chapels housing family tombs were built along the right-hand side of the building. The top of the transept has retained its 13th-century appearance; the campanile dates from the 14th century.

The brick facade was restored by Maciachini in Lombard Gothic style in 1871; the middle portal with its pointed arch and architrave decorated with scenes from the Life of Christ, symbols of the Evangelists and two saints (14th century), is part of the structure that originally stood on the site. Three niches above the portal contain statues of saints Mark, Ambrose and Augustine.

San Marco fresco

The baroque interior dates from 1694. The family chapels in the right-hand side-aisle contain some fine paintings, and the right transept, with all its tomb inscriptions and monuments, is of particular interest – especially the sarcophagus of St Lanfranco da Settala (died 1264), a work by Giovanni di Balduccio.

To the right of the main altar in the apse is the large painting *Dispute Between SS Ambrose and Augstine* (17th century) by Camillo Procaccini, and on the left-hand side is the *Baptism of St Augustine* (1618) by Cerano. On the left-hand side of the left transept is the Cappella della Pietà with its *Entombment of Christ* altarpiece (a copy in the style of Caravaggio).

From Piazza San Marco, Via Pontaccio leads on to a right turn down Via San Simpliciano. Soon the Piazza Crociate comes into view, with its ancient church of **San Simpliciano ㉒**, one of the most beautiful churches in Milan

San Simpliciano

(Monday to Friday 7am–noon and 3–7pm, Saturday and Sunday 8am–noon and 4–7pm). It was probably founded by St Ambrose in the 4th century on the site of an ancient Roman cemetery and completed by Ambrose's successor, St Simplician, who also lies buried here. Despite alterations over the centuries, the church has retained its Romanesque appearance; the campanile, however, was considerably reduced in height at the request of the Spanish government, since it used to be higher than the nearby Castello Sforzesco, which lay within firing distance. Concerts are often held here and in San Marco.

It was from San Simpliciano during the time of the medieval commune that the *Carroccio*, Milan's flagwagon, used to depart for battle. Legend has it that on the day of the battle of Legnano (fought between the Lombard League and Emperor Frederick Barbarossa, 29 May 1176), three white doves flew out of the room in the church where the relics of three martyrs – Martirio, Sisinio and Alessandro – were kept; apparently they landed on the flagpoles and helped the communes on to victory. To commemorate the great occasion, balloons are released on 29 May every year in the square in front of the church.

The Wise and Foolish Virgins

The Wise and Foolish Virgins from the Gospel of St Matthew can be seen on the capitals of the central portal (12th century) in the facade. Traces of the Early Christian structure can still be clearly seen on the side walls of the three-aisled interior. The large ★ *Coronation of the Vir-*

Exterior mosaic

gin fresco in the apse (c 1515, by Ambrogio da Fossano, called Bergognone) depicts God the Father embracing the Virgin and Jesus. The altar slab (beneath the neoclassical *baldacchino*) is a 5th- or 6th-century marble parapet. The statues of the saints on the organ loft are by Aurelio Luini, son of the great Bernardino. On the left, opposite the sacristy, is the remarkable altarpiece *Marriage of the Virgin* (17th century) by Procaccini. The painted glass on the inner wall of the facade (1927) is based on designs by Aldo Carpi and was executed by Trevarotto; it depicts episodes from the battle of Legnano.

Relaxing on the church steps

39

To visit the cloisters, contact the *Facoltà Teologica Interregionale dell'Italia Settentrionale* (the porter's lodge is at house No 6; Tuesday to Friday 9am–1pm and 2–6pm, Monday by appointment; closed Saturday, Sunday and holidays). Past a Renaissance cloister dating from 1449 is the *Chiostro delle due colonne*, a two-storeyed structure with double columns. It was built in the 16th century.

From the Piazza Crociate, continue along the Corso Garibaldi; the route passes through a typically Milanese part of the city as far as the Largo la Foppa (Metro line 2, Moscova), where there is a monument to G G Piatti, inventor of the pneumatic drill. From here you can walk along the Via Volta and the Viale Ceresio (or take a No 61 bus) to reach the Cimitero Monumentale (*see page 40*).

One detour that is particularly worthwhile, however, is to take the route via the church of **Santa Maria Incoronata** ㉓. This actually comprises two churches, built next to each other in the 15th century and sharing several Gothic features. The left-hand church was commissioned in 1451 by Francesco Sforza, and the right-hand one nine years later by his wife, Maria Visconti; the double facade is decorated with a pilaster bearing the arms of the Visconti family. Several important members of the Sforza court lie buried here.

Santa Maria Incoronata

At the end of the Corso Garibaldi is a triumphal arch, erected in 1825 in honour of Austrian Emperor Francis I, and then dedicated to freedom-fighter Garibaldi in 1859. The route now continues left down the Viale Francesco Crispi and then right at the Piazza Baiamonti, taking the Via Ceresio as far as the **Cimitero Monumentale ㉔** (April to September 8.30am–5.15pm; October to March 8.30am–4.30pm; closed Monday).This cemetery covers around 200,000sq m (239,200sq yds) and contains countless tombstones, monuments and chapels, many of them superb works of art. Designed in the Lombard Gothic style by Carlo Maciachini and opened in 1860, it has often been described as a Sculpture Museum. The large building at the centre of the cemetery facade is known as the *Famedio* (Temple of Honour) and is dedicated to several famous Milanese; those buried here include the poet Alessandro Manzoni and the writer Carlo Cattaneo, who initiated the *Cinque Giornate* uprising of 1848.

Cimitero Monumentale

Take a No 29 or 30 tram now as far as the Piazzale Principessa Clotilde, then walk along the Corso Porta Nuova as far as the Piazza Sant'Angelo, and the church of **Sant 'Angelo ㉕** (Sunday to Friday 6.30am–8pm, closed Saturday). This Franciscan church was built in Late Renaissance style by Domenico Giunti in 1552. The interior radiates monastic austerity and simplicity. The adjacent monastery has been the seat of the Franciscan Order here since 1730.

Sant' Angelo

Next to the church is the entrance to the so-called *Angelicum*, an exhibition centre. In the Piazza Sant'Angelo is the Fountain of St Francis (1927, by Giannino Castiglioni), a real favourite with the Milanese: the saint is shown speaking to the pigeons on the edge of the fountain and the fish splashing inside it.

The Corso Porta Nuova and the Via dell'Annunciata now lead to the **Archi di Porta Nuova ㉖**. The Porta Nuova is one of the city gates from the wall built by Barbarossa between 1156 and 1158. Set into the facade

40

facing inwards to the city are two Roman tombstones; on the other facade is a large marble tabernacle (14th century, probably the work of Giovanni di Balduccio) with a statue of the Virgin. Inside the arch the grooves for the portcullis are clearly visible.

The Giardini Pubblici

Beyond the Porta Nuova is the busy traffic junction of the **Piazza Cavour**, surrounded by a number of modern building complexes, eg the 78-m (255-ft) high Swiss Centre skyscraper (1952). The monument to Cavour stands in the background. Next to it is the entrance to the most important open space in the city, the ★ **Giardini Pubblici**. This park between the Piazza Cavour and the Porta Venezia covers an area of almost 177,000sq m (211,600sq yds) and was originally laid out in 1782 by Piermarini, who made use of the grounds of former monasteries. The gardens were given their present-day appearance in 1858 by Giuseppe Balzaretti, who laid them out in the English romantic style, with bushes, small hills, ponds and an abundance of exotic plants.

Statue of Cavour

To the west is the **Palazzo Dugnani [A]**, the main hall of which is decorated with frescoes by Giovanni Battista (Giambattista) Tiepolo, and it also contains the Museo del Cinema. The ★ **Museo Civico di Storia Naturale** (Natural History Museum) **[B]** was founded in 1838 and is housed inside a Neo-Romanesque/Gothic building dating from 1893 (Monday to Friday 9am–6pm, Saturday, Sunday and holidays 9.30am–6.30pm; admission free). The ground floor contains mineral collections and palaeontological exhibits; highlights of the museum include a huge 40-kilo (88-lb) topaz, a collection of meteorites and a dinosaur skeleton. The zoological collection and the library are on the first floor.

From the insect collection

To the east, past the children's playground **[C]** and the famous Planetarium **[D]**, is the Metro station of Porta Venezia (line 1).

41

Garibaldi

Route 4

Castello Sforzesco – Parco Sempione

This route begins on the Largo Cairoli, a square surrounded by some very elegant 19th-century houses; at its southern end is the little Church of Santa Maria delle Consolazione. It was built in the 16th century; the facade was added later, in the 19th century.

In the centre of the square is an equestrian statue of Giuseppe Garibaldi (1895, by Ettore Ximenes). To the east and west of the square are the two arms of the Foro Buonaparte, a generously-proportioned avenue planned in 1801, during the period of the Cisalpine Republic, but built between 1886 and 1889.

The rather short Via Beltrami leads into the Piazza Castello, which formerly contained the outworks of the ★★ **Castello Sforzesco** ❷❼ (open 9am–5.45pm daily), which were dismantled by Napoleon Bonaparte. This huge

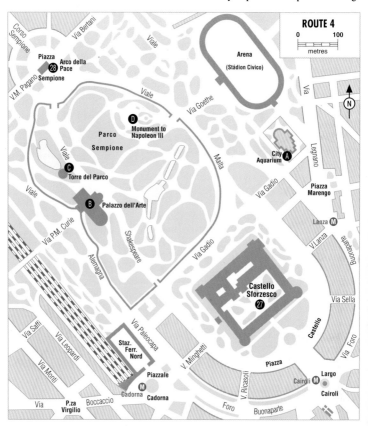

complex of brick buildings is not only of architectural interest: it also contains several superb art collections.

The Castello is the former castle of the Sforza and Visconti families. Originally it was known as the Castello di Porta Giovia, after a small gate in the medieval city wall that was later built into the castle walls. The western section, or Rocchetta, was laid out as a fortress in 1368 by Galeazzo II Visconti; it was partially destroyed by the people of Milan during the riots that followed the death of the last Visconti in 1447, but then rebuilt by Francesco Sforza from 1450 onwards; he also extended the original building considerably, adding the Corte Ducale as well as the Cortile delle Milizie. The construction work was supervised by Giovanni da Milano, Filippo Scorzioli, Jacopo di Cortona, Filarete from Florence and Bartolomeo Gadio from Cremona (in that order). Francesco's son Galeazzo Maria and his widow Bona of Savoy completed the extension work to the castle between 1466 and 1477.

Castle gardener

Lodovico il Moro (1480–99) commissioned artists such as Leonardo da Vinci and Bramante to do further work on the Castello, which by then was one of the greatest Italian castles of the period, with accommodation for 800 courtiers and servants. In 1521 an explosion caused by gunpowder destroyed Filarete's gate-tower leading to the **Cortile delle Milizie** (restored according to the original plans in 1905). From the Spanish occupation onwards the castle was used as a fortress; its fortifications were razed by Napoleon I. In 1893 the city of Milan had the castle restored in 15th-century style by Luca Beltrami; after World War II the complex was restored yet again. The Musei del Castello Sforzesco can be found in the former Corte Ducale and in the Rocchetta. Only a few of the exhibition halls are open to the public.

The Cortile delle Milizie

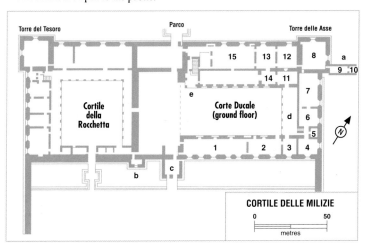

Torre dell'Orologio

At the centre of the facade on the Piazza Castello is the huge quadrilateral Torre dell'Orologio (clock-tower, also known as the Torre Umberto I or Torre di Filarete). This 70-m (250-ft) high, tapering tower (1905) is a copy of the gate added by Filarete in the 15th century. A bas-relief above the portal (1905, by Luigi Secchi) shows Umberto I on horseback; above is a statue of St Ambrose, flanked by six ducal coats-of-arms of the Sforza family.

At either end of the facade, which is broken up by elegant double-arched brick windows, are two rusticated round towers. They are 31m (100ft) high and bear huge marble coats-of-arms showing the snake, symbol of the Sforza and Visconti families. Since 1897 the towers have been in use as part of treatment facilities for the city's sewage system.

On the left-hand side of the outer wall is the Porta Santo Spirito, which forms the connection with the medieval city walls. Nearby are the picturesque ruins of the Rivellino Santo Spirito, a former bastion. The wall of the castle here feature some single- or double-arched Gothic window.

The Ponticella
Tower of Bona of Savoy

On the right-hand side of the outer wall are the Porta dei Carmini, with a drawbridge, and just beyond it, Lodovico il Moro's **Ponticella [a]**, with a delightful 15th-century loggia by Bramante above it, which once connected the Castello with the outer fortifications. The facade, facing the Parco has square corner-towers.

The Cortile delle Milizie (also known as the Piazza d'Armi) is reached via the above-mentioned clock-tower. Across to the left is the Rocchetta, to which the dukes would retire whenever danger threatened. Almost at the centre of the courtyard facade is the huge 36-m (118-ft) high **Tower of Bona of Savoy [b]**, built in 1477. To the

right are the buildings of the Corte Ducale, containing the ducal apartments; the outlines of the former windows can still be picked out in the brickwork. In front of the moat is a statue of St John of Nepomuk (1729). Remains of earlier structures, which date from the 16th century, can be made out on the right-hand side of the facade in the main courtyard.

St John of Nepomuk

Beyond the Cortile delle Milizie we now pass through a square **gate [c]**, built on the site of the former Porta Giovia and bearing the Sforza arms as well as a *Crucifixion* fresco by an anonymous Lombard artist (c 1470). This leads to the courtyard of the ducal residence proper, surrounded on three sides by one-storey buildings with two rows of pointed-arch windows.

The arcade at the rear of the courtyard is called the **Portico dell'Elefante [d]** after a fresco of an elephant there; it was built in 1473 by Benedetto Ferrini, who was also responsible for Galeazzo Sforza's delightful **loggia [e]** at the foot of the Scala d'Onore (Staircase of Honour).

The Portico dell'Elefante

Through the square gate **[c]** on the right (*see above*) is the entrance to the **Sforza Castle Art Galleries** (Tuesday to Sunday 9.30am–5.30pm; closed Monday, New Year's Day, Easter, 1 May, 15 August and Christmas; admission free).

The first museum you come to is the ★ **Civici Musei d'Arte**. Only the most important exhibits in the museum's 26 halls can be mentioned here (*see plans on pages 43 and 48*). The entrance hall contains the so-called *Pusterla dei fabbri*, remains of the Visconti's wall from the 14th century. The halls on the ground floor contain an assortment of Lombard sculpture.

Fragments of history

1 Early Christian and Pre-Romanesque art, eg fragments of mosaic pavements, tomb frescoes, the remains of buildings, capitals, sarcophagi, etc (4th–9th century).

2 Romanesque art, with reliefs and remains of buildings dating from the 12th century; a 13th-century wooden crucifix; and the tomb monument of Regina della Scala, wife of Bernabò Visconti (14th-century). The hall is dominated by the tomb and equestrian statue of Bernabò Visconti (1370–80, by Bonino da Campione), which stood originally in the Church of San Giovanni in Conca. In the lunettes and along the rear wall of the hall are the coats-of-arms of various Spanish city governors.

3 Ceiling fresco of the *Resurrection* (15th century, artist unknown); statue of Jacob the Elder (14th century); front of the sarcophagus of Fra Mirano di Bachaloe (14th century); votive statues of the Virgin that once adorned the city's former gates

(14th century, school of Giovanni di Balduccio); also the tomb-slab (1438) of Antonello Arcimboldi.

4 On the ceiling, a coat-of-arms depicting the emblems of Philip II of Spain and his wife Mary Tudor (1555); several fragments from the church facade of Santa Maria di Brera (14th century, by Giovanni di Balduccio); stone slab with a *Pietà* (14th century, Campione school); tomb slab of the Rusca family (14th-century Lombard); and a wall-fresco of the *Annunciation* (14th century, from San Giovanni in Conca).

5 *Headless Madonna* (14th-century statuette by Giovanni Pisano); alabaster relief of *The Kiss of Judas* (14th century, English); on the floor, tomb-slab of Giovanni Lanfranchini (14th century).

6 Exhibits documenting Milanese history, including bas-reliefs of the former Porta Romana, depicting the expulsion of the Arians by St Ambrose and also the triumphal return of the Milanese after the battle of Legnano against Barbarossa (12th century, by Anselmo and Gherardo da Campione).

46 *17th-century tapestries*

7 On the walls: Lombard and Flemish tapestries (17th century); in the middle of the hall, the banner of Milan (1566, by Giuseppe Meda) with embroidered scenes from the life of St Ambrose.

8 This hall (which is also known as the Sala delle Asse because of its former 15th-century panelling) was furnished with frescoes by Leonardo da Vinci in 1498. The frescoes depict a mock balcony with trees (and the arms of Lodovico il Moro); the restoration work here was carried out by Ernesto Rusca in 1902.

9 This hall (known as the Saletta Negra) was often used by Lodovico il Moro for meditation and contemplation after the death of his wife, Beatrice d'Este; it, too, was once decorated by Leonardo, though all that remains of his work today is a panel with the inscription: 'Everything that Mortals Consider as Happy is Finally Sad'. On the walls are medallion portraits of the Sforza (early 16th century) by Bernardino Luini; the tomb sculptures (16th century) are by Bambaia.

10 More portraits of the Sforza by Bernardino Luini.

11 The fresco in the vaulted ceiling of this former audience chamber, the Sala dei Ducali, bears the arms of the Sforza dynasty and the initials of Galeazzo Maria (GZ), above which Lodovico il Moro had his own placed (LU). The hall contains several Late-Gothic sculptures, including a bas-relief with allegorical scenes (14th century, by Agostino di Duccio) from the Malatesta Chapel in

Rimini, and also angels (15th century) by Michelino da Firenze, in two niches.

12. The Cappella Ducale was built between 1472 and 1473 by Benedetto Ferrini, who received the commission from Galeazzo Maria. The *Resurrection* fresco on the ceiling and the saints on the walls are by Stefano de Fedeli and his pupils. In the middle of the room is a *Madonna in Prayer* (15th century) attributed to Pietro Solari.

The Resurrection fresco

13. The so-called Sala delle Colombine (Hall of the Doves) is named after the fresco decoration depicting doves, commissioned by Bona of Savoy. The room also contains several different Lombard sculptures (15th century), and two angels (16th century) by Amadeo.

14. The Sala Verde (it was once coloured green) contains the castle's weapon collection and several magnificent Renaissance portals (including the portal belonging to the Medici Bank in Milan, 1455, by Michelozzo).

15. The Sala degli Scarlioni is named after the zigzag decoration in the Sforza colours that was used to decorate the walls. This is where the Secret Council used to meet. The hall consists of two rooms: in the first is the funerary statue of Gaston de Foix (1525) by Agostino Busti, called Bambaia, and the large tomb monument to Bishop Baragoto (1519, by Andrea Fusina). A broad staircase leads to the other room, containing the unfinished ★★ **Pietà Rondanini**, Michelangelo's last work and named after its original location in Palazzo Rondanini.

The Pietá Rondanini
Knight in shining armour

47

A wooden walkway along some battlements crosses the Cortile della Fontana (containing a fine marble copy of an old Sforza fountain and some attractive brick windows); then an old stairway (Scala Cavallina) on the right leads to the upper floors (*see plan below*).

16–19   These first four halls contain a furniture collection comprising some 600 items; only the most attractive pieces are actually on display. Most of the furniture is domestic, from Northern Italy. Hall 17 also contains a fresco cycle from the Castello Roccabianca near Parma, depicting Griseldi's story from Boccaccio's *Decameron*.

Pinacoteca artworks

The remainder of the halls are devoted to the ★**Picture Gallery** (Pinacoteca). Most of the works here are by Lombard masters of various periods.

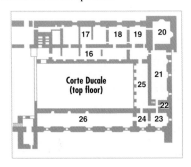

20   The Sala Dorata, containing Late-Gothic and Early-Renaissance works by various schools, including *Madonna in Humility* by Filippo Lippi; *Madonna and Child* by Giovanni Bellini; *Madonna in Glory* (1497) by Andrea Mantegna; and works by Lorenzo Veneziano and Carlo Crivelli.

21   16th-century paintings, notably by Il Bergognone (*Pietà*; three paintings of *St Benedict, St Hieronymus* and *St Roche*); Vincenzo Foppa (*S. Augustine* and *Theodore*; *Madonna with Book*); Bernardino Luini (*Madonna*); and works by Boltraffio, Sodoma, Romanino, Moretto, Bramantino and Correggio.

22   This small room next door contains a number of Mannerist paintings.

23   Lombard paintings from the Cappella del Tribunale di Provvisione di Milano a Santa Marta in the Palazzo dei Giureconsulti.

24   This hall contains works by various exponents of Lombard Mannerism, including Bernadino Campi, Giuseppe Arcimboldi and Cesare Procaccini.

25   The Lombard Room. For alternating exhibitions.

26 17th-century and 18th-century masters, including paintings by Magnasco (*Market*, and two storm pictures), by Francesco Guardi, Jusepe Ribera *(St Hieronymus)* and Tiepolo.

Courtyard of the Rochetta

A small bridge now crosses the upper section of the Bona of Savoy Tower and leads into the upper rooms of the **Rocchetta** containing the Civiche Raccolte d'Arte Applicata (Museum of Applied Art); halls **33** to **38** here contain fine gold and ivory work and also valuable blown glass from Murano. There is a magnificent gold Gothic monstrance dating from 1456, and the *Virgin at the Tomb* series of small, carved ivory panels (Romanesque, 5th century) are also of particular interest.

The halls on the ground floor contain a collection of old textiles, leather goods and paraments (wall hangings), and also a Musical Instrument Museum. This contains around 650 exhibits (including violins by Gasparo da Salò and Guarneri) and is the most comprehensive museum of its kind in Europe. On the same floor is the Sala della Balla (usually closed since it is used for civic receptions); which has 12 allegorical tapestries of the months (the so-called *Trivulzio* tapestries, named after the Milanese nobleman who commissioned them). They were created in 1503 according to designs by Bramantino.

One of 650 exhibits

The courtyard of the Rocchetta is surrounded on three sides by arcaded walkways dating from the late 15th century. Artists who worked on them include Benedetto Ferini, Filarete, Bernardino da Corte and Bramante; the medallions contain several different coats-of-arms of the Visconti and Sforza families. The courtyard leads to the treasury *(tesoro),* where the ducal treasure was once kept. There is a remarkable fresco here of the 100-eyed *Argus* by Bramante (15th century). Beneath it a small door leads to a room where the most valuable items were kept.

The Prehistoric and Egyptian collections are on the basement floor. The Prehistoric Collection includes archaeological finds from Palaeolithic times to the Iron Age. The sections of lake dwellings from the Lagozza di Besnate are particularly interesting, as are the remains of the Golasecca culture (Iron Age) and the Celtic finds. The small Egyptian Collection includes sarcophagi, mummies, steles, tomb statues, jewellery and other burial items.

Forward planning

Leave the Castello Sforzesco by its northwest gate, the *Porta del Barco*; on the other side of the moat is ★ **Parco Sempione** (daily 6.30am–8pm, later in Summer).This English-style park, 47 hectares (116 acres) in size, was laid out in 1893 according to plans by Emilio Alemagna.

Aquarium tilework

On the right is the **City Aquarium [A]** (daily 9.30am–5.30pm) and beyond it the *Arena*, or *Stadio Civico*, which was modelled on the stadia of antiquity by Luigi Canonica, and opened in the presence of Napoleon I in 1807. Originally built to host horse- and coach-races as well as mock naval battles, the arena is used for sports events as well as the occasional musical show, and can accommodate around 30,000 spectators. The longitudinal axis (238m/780ft) lies between the *Porta Trionfale* and the *Porta delle Carceri*, where the coaches and horses were formerly kept. The broadest part of the arena extends from the *Pulvinare* (Princes' Box) and the *Porta Libitinaria*, recalling the gravediggers of the Roman amphitheatres who had to drag dying gladiators out of similar gates.

50

In the western part of the park is the **Palazzo dell'Arte [B]**, built in 1933 and the permanent headquarters of the Milan *Triennale* (Tuesday to Sunday 10am–8pm, closed Monday). It stages important exhibitions organised by the Triennale, including architecture and design, town planning, decorative arts and fashion.

Not far away is the 108-m (340-ft) high iron viewing tower known as the **Torre del Parco [C]**. On the hill of Monte Tondo there is a **monument [D]** to Napoleon III.

Arco della Pace relief

At the end of the park is the Piazzale Sempione, with its **Arco della Pace ㉘**. This Roman-style triumphal arch in honour of Napoleon Bonaparte, designed by Cagnola, was begun in 1807. In 1826, the Austrian Emperor Francis I dedicated it to the memory of the 1815 Congress of Vienna as an Arch of Peace. Since 1859 the arch has stood as a reminder of the triumphal march into the city by the Piedmontese-French troops under Victor Emmanuel II and Napoleon III. The neoclassical arch is 25m (82ft) high and 24m (80ft) wide. On the attic is a bronze statue with six horses representing peace (by Abbondio Sangiorgio) and four goddesses of victory on horseback (by Giovanni Putti). At the very top are allegorical depictions of the main rivers of Lombardy and Venetia: the Po, the Ticino, the Adige and the Tagliamento.

Route 5

Piazzale Cadorna – Sant'Ambrogio

To the southwest of the Castello Sforzesco (*see page 42*), in front of the North Station, is the elongated Piazzale Cadorna (*see map, page 42*). From here, take the Via Carducci as far as the Corso Magenta, turn left into the latter, passing the **Palazzo Litta** (1648, by Richini; rococo facade added in 1763), and a little further on is the church of **San Maurizio**  (Monday to Friday 4–6pm, Sunday 10.30–11.30am). Also known as the Chiesa del Monastero Maggiore, this building was once the monastery church of a powerful Benedictine convent. The present structure, designed by Bramantino, was erected between 1503 and 1519 by Giacomo Dolcebuono and Cristoforo Solari. The unpretentious facade dates from 1574–81; the gable on top is a baroque addition.

The interior of the church consists of a nave with a row of chapels on either side, and a series of dwarf galleries in the upper section. A high wall (*see diagram, page 52*) separates the front section of the church (reserved for the congregation) from the rear section (which was

Detail, Palazzo Litta

San Maurizio

51

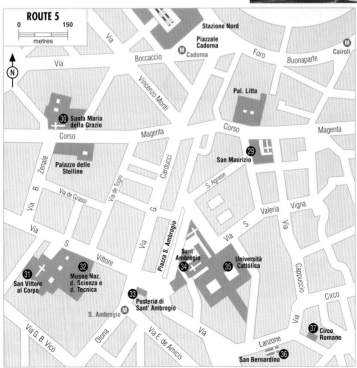

ROUTE 5

0   150
metres

N

Stazione Nord

Piazzale Cadorna

Via Boccaccio

Cadorna

Foro Buonaparte

Cairoli

Via

Vincenzo Monti

Pal. Litta

Santa Maria delle Grazie

Corso Magenta

Corso

Magenta

Zenale

Palazzo delle Stelline

Carducci

San Maurizio

S. Agnese

Via B.

Via de Grassi

Via de Togni

G.

Valeria

Vigna

Via

S.

Via

Via

S.

Sant' Ambrogio

Vittore

Piazza S. Ambrogio

Sant' Ambrogio

Università Cattólica

Cappuccio

San Vittore al Corpo

Museo Naz. d. Scienza e d. Tecnica

Pusteria di Sant' Ambrogio

Circo

Circo Romano

Via G. B. Vico

Olona

S. Ambrogio

Via E. de Amicis

Via

Lanzone

Via

San Bernardino

SAN MAURIZIO

formerly reserved for the nuns). The walls in both sections of the church and the partition wall are completely covered with frescoes.

To the left and right of the entry portal are the frescoes depicting two New Testament scenes: the parable of the *Return of the Prodigal Son* and *Expulsion of the Moneylenders from the Temple* (16th century) by Simone Peterzano. The second chapel on the left contains frescoes and also an *Entombment* (1555) by Callisto Piazza; the third chapel on the right contains the last works by Bernardino Luini: frescoes portraying scenes from the life of St Catherine of Alexandria (1530). The frescoes on the partition wall (1522) are also by Luini.

a *SS Cecilia and Ursula*
b *Alessandro Bentivoglio with S. Placidus, Benedict and John the Baptist*
c *Martyrdom of St Maurice*
d *Assumption of the Virgin*
e *St Sigismund Presents St Maurice with a Model of the Church*
f *Ippolita Sforza, Wife of Bentivoglio, with Three Female Saints*
g *St Apollonia, the Resurrected Christ and St Lucy*

The *Adoration of the Magi* [h] decorating the main altar is by Antonio Campi. In the fourth chapel on the left is the passageway leading to the nuns' choir; the choir stalls have been attributed to Dolcebuono.

On the other side of the partition are further frescoes by Luini, this time featuring angels and saints as well as several scenes from the Passion: one of the onlookers in the *Deposition* fresco (located above the entrance portal on the right-hand side) is meant to be Bianca Bentivoglio dressed in a nun's habit.

A small stairway behind the choir leads to the upper cloister with some delightful statues of female saints in 26 medallions (1505–10, by Boltraffio).

The towers beyond the apse are believed to be Roman in origin; the square one probably belonged to the prison at the Circus Maximus, and the polygonal one was part of a defensive wall built during the reign of the Emperor Maximilian.

Museum courtyard

To the right of the church of San Maurizio is the entrance to the former *Monastero Maggiore*, which today houses the **Archaeological Museum** (Tuesday to Sunday 9.30am–5.30pm; closed New Year's Day, Easter, 1 May, 15 August and Christmas; admission free).

Now take the Corso Magenta in a westerly direction, passing the Case Atellani (house Nos 65 and 67), both of them typical 15th-century structures. On the opposite side of the street is the silhouette of the magnificent church of ★★ **Santa Maria delle Grazie** ⑳. This church was built in a Gothic-Renaissance transitional style between 1465 and 1490 by Guiniforte Solari; a new apse and cupola were added soon afterwards by Bramante, who received the commission from Lodovico il Moro. Bramante also constructed the magnificent marble portal in the facade.

Santa Maria delle Grazie inside (below) and out (above)

The three-aisled interior (partly under restoration) has 15th-century fresco decoration in its groined vault, and the copestones on the ribs are decorated with reliefs of saints. On the pilasters in the side-aisles and in the lunettes of the nave there are several pictures of beatified Dominicans (15th century, by Butinone).

A Tombs of noblemen (15th–16th century) and a *Madonna* at the altar (15th century).

B Frescoes of the *Passion* (1540) by Gaudenzio Ferrari.

C Votive fresco depicting *Madonna, Saints and the Founder* (1517, Leonardo da Vinci school).

53

D Little Cloister by Bramante; above the entrance, *St Peter Martyr and St Catherine*, and above the door to the sacristy, *St Peter Martyr and Louis of Toulouse*, both by Bramantino (16th century).

E Sacristy, also by Bramante, with painted cabinets (1489) and a valuable clock dating from 1680.

F *Cappella della Madonna delle Grazie* with the much-revered altarpiece *Our Lady of Mercy with the Vimercati Family* (15th century).

G Great Cloister by Solari, which was reconstructed in the style of 1463 after bomb damage during the war.

Great Cloister

H Tomb of Cardinal Luigi Arcimboldi (16th century, by Bambaia) and the tomb-slab of Count Branda Castiglioni (15th century, attributed to Amadeo).

Next to the church is the entrance to the Cenacolo Vinciano, the refectory ★★★ **Last Supper** by Leonardo da Vinci (Tuesday to Friday and Sunday 8.15am–6.45pm, Saturday 8.15am–10.15pm, closed Monday, admission fee; it is strongly advisable to book at least three days in advance, as tickets are usually sold out if you arrive without a reservation, tel: 02-89421146). This fresco, commissioned from Leonardo by Lodovico il Moro and painted between 1495 and 1497 covers the entire rear wall of the former refectory of this Dominican monastery; it is 9m (30ft) long and 4½m (14ft) high. Leonardo did

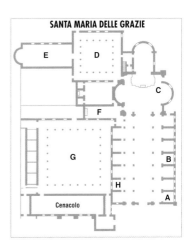

SANTA MARIA DELLE GRAZIE

The Last Supper

not use the traditional techniques of fresco painting here, but instead employed a technique he had developed: tempera on a base mixed by himself on the stone wall. This procedure proved unsuccessful: the base began to loosen from the wall, and inadequate restoration work from the 17th to the 19th century only made it worse. The rear of the wall was heated in 1908, but made no noticeable difference. In 1943 the refectory was destroyed in a bombing raid, but the *Last Supper* remained unscathed. The most recent restoration on the work was completed in 1999, but there has been much criticism of the result – although true to the original, it is somewhat lacklustre.

Leonardo's masterpiece portrays the moment when Jesus tells his disciples: 'One of you shall betray me.' The power of this painting derives from the striking contrast in the attitudes of the 12 disciples as counterposed to Christ; they are agitated, while Christ sits in transfigured serenity. Judas is clearly the guilty figure of the company. The monumental simplicity of this fresco is quite masterful, and reflects Leonardo's lifetime maxim of *Saper vedere* – 'knowing how to see'.

On the opposite wall is a fresco of the *Crucifixion* (1495, by Donato da Montorfano) containing the faint figures, added by Leonardo, of Lodovico il Moro and his family.

Continue along Via Zenale, then turn left down Via S Vittore to reach the church of **San Vittore al Corpo** ③ (Monday to Saturday 7.30am–noon and 3.30–7pm, Sunday 8am–1pm). It was built in its present form by Galeazzo Alessi in 1560. The interior contains 17th-century stucco work and frescoes, and some fine 16th-century choir stalls.

Next door is the former monastery of San Vittore; today it houses the **Museo Nazionale della Scienza e Tecnica** ③ (Tuesday to Friday 9.30am–4.50pm, Saturday and Sunday 9.30am–6.30pm; closed Monday; admission fee). Among the collections documenting the History of Tech-

Da Vinci drawing

nology are Leonardo's actual ★ models, which cast light on his plans and studies of fortifications, submarines, etc.

The **Pusterla di Sant'Ambrogio** ㉝ is an old sally-port built into the city wall in 1167, which was later used as a prison and today contains the **Museum of Criminology and Antique Weapons** (daily 10am–7.30pm). The figures dating from 1360 above the arches depict saints Ambrose, Gervase and Protasius.

Directly opposite is the entrance to the church of ★★ **Sant'Ambrogio** ㉞ (daily 7am–noon and 2.30–7pm). It was built by St Ambrose between 379 and 387 to house the relics of the martyrs Gervase and Protasius. Altered in the 9th and 12th century, the basilica is the epitome of the Lombard Romanesque style. St Ambrose was buried here in 387; his tomb is in the crypt. Between the 8th and 14th century, nine emperors were crowned in Sant' Ambrogio with the famous 'iron crown of the Lombards'.

Sant'Ambrogio

A Rectangular atrium (1150) on an Early Christian plan, surrounded by large arcades. The capitals on the columns are decorated with symbolic animals, acanthus leaves, centaurs and other mythological creatures. Below the arcades is a lapidarium containing Roman and Romanesque capitals, tombstones, and pagan and Early Christian inscriptions; there are also the remains of some frescoes on the walls (12th–13th century).

B Campanile dei Monaci (Monks' Tower), 9th century.

C Campanile dei Canonici (Canons' Tower), built 1128–1144 in order to end a dispute about church-bells between the canons and the Benedictine monks from the neighbouring monastery. The tower is 43.5m (143ft) high, and has a fine loggia (1889).

St Ambrose fresco

D The facade of the church consists of two superimposed loggie, the upper one of which has five arcades. The lower hall has three portals; the centre one is framed by narrow columns and Romanesque decoration. The doors, beautifully carved in cypress wood (4th–9th century) underwent extensive restoration during the 18th century. The great bronze door-knockers are Lombard (8th–9th century); the side portals with their massive architraves show likenesses of animals. On the left of the main portal is the marble tomb of the humanist Pier Candido Decembrio (1447, by Tomaso Cazzaniga).

E There are three early 13th-century frescoes on the piers: *St Ambrose*, *Virgin and Child*, and *The Founder Bonamico Taverna*.

F Antique columns with a bronze serpent (10th-century Byzantine) – according to legend, that of Moses.

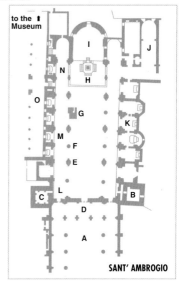
to the ↑ Museum

SANT' AMBROGIO

The Last Supper relief

G Pulpit *(Ambo)* originally built in the 11th century, and rebuilt after it collapsed in 1201. The Last Supper relief on the front dates from the 11th century; the bronze eagle and angel are over a century older.

Beneath the pulpit is an Early Christian sarcophagus (4th-century), which is said to contain the remains of Stilicho and his wife Serena; he was a general in the army of Emperor Theodosius the Great. The central relief on the sarcophagus depicts *Christ and the Scholars*; to the right of it *Elijah and his Chariot of Fire* and *Noah and Moses*; on the back, *Christ and the Apostles*, and to the left, *The Sacrifice of Abraham*.

H On the high altar is a notable ★ altar casing by the German goldsmith Volvinius (9th century). The front shows the Redeemer, the symbols of the Evangelists, the Apostles and the Life of Christ; on the back are scenes from the life of St Ambrose.

Above the altar is the ★ ciborium (9th century). The baldachin is decorated with gilt and polychrome stucco (Lombard-Byzantine, 9th century); clockwise from the front it depicts *Christ Giving the Keys to Peter and the Book to Paul*, *The Virgin and Two Worshippers*, *SS Ambrose, Gervase and Protasius Receiving the Model of the Ciborium*, and *St Benedict with Two Believers*.

I Around the raised apse are several sections off the double row of choir stalls dating from the 16th century, with carvings depicting scenes from the life of St Ambrose; at the centre is a marble episcopal chair (9th century). The mosaics in the apse (6th–19th century) depict: *Christ with SS Gervase and Protasius*; on the left, *St Ambrose at the Burial of St Martin of Tours*; and on the right, *SS Ambrose and Augustine*.

Beneath the choir is the **crypt**. The first room was decorated in the baroque style in the 18th century; the second contains a silver shrine (1898) containing the relics of SS Ambrose, Gervase and Protasius. At the back of the room is a porphyry sarcophagus in which the relics were discovered in 1864, and the *Colonna della Pietà*, which once stood in the Piazza Castello to mark the site of the martyrdom of Gervase and Protasius.

J *Sacello di San Vittore in Ciel d'Oro* (5th century) with a Byzantine mosaic on a gold background from the end of the 5th century; on the ceiling is St Victor, with (to the right of him) SS Felix, Maternus and Nabor, and to the left, SS Ambrose, Gervase and Protasius.

K *Cappella della Santa Sevina*, with an Early Christian sarcophagus (5th century; scenes from the Passion) acting as an altarpiece.

L On the architrave above the doors, *Putti Picking Grapes*, a rare work dating from the 5th or 6th century. A little further on, the baptistry has a *Resurrection* fresco by Bergognone (1491) behind its (modern) font, and in the vault is the fresco *Paradise* by Isidoro Bianchi.

M At the altar in the chapel is a round painting of the *Madonna* by Luini.

N Tomb-slab of *Pippin*, second son of Charlemagne.

O Portico della Canonica, a section of the cloister that was begun by Bramante in 1492 and never completed. The brick building in front of it is the 10th-century Oratorio di San Sigismondo. In the middle of the arcade there are relief busts of Lodovico il Moro and his wife Beatrice d'Este (late 15th century).

Artist at work
Sant' Ambrogio cloister

Here is the entrance to the fascinating ★ **Museo della Basilica di Sant'Ambrogio** (daily except Tuesday 10am–noon and 3–5pm; Saturday, Sunday and public holidays 3–5pm; closed New Year's Day, Easter, 1 May, 15 August and Christmas; admission fee). This museum contains several priceless antiquities and the treasure from the Basilica of St Ambrose. The exhibits include the work of goldsmiths from the 12th to the 16th century; the dalmatic (ecclesiastical robe) of St Ambrose; the saint's bedframe; fragments from the oldest portal of the basilica (4th–9th century); Flemish tapestries (17th century); and more than 1,000 manuscripts.

In the middle of the Piazza Sant'Ambrogio is the Tempio della Vittoria (1928, by Muzio), commemorating the Milanese who fell during World War I. At the southern end of the square is the Colonna del Diavolo, an antique column, which derives its name from its two holes – legend has it that they were left by the devil's horns when he angrily discovered that St Ambrose was not to be tempted.

Beyond the basilica is the **Università Cattólica** ㉟. Founded in 1921, the Catholic University is housed in a Benedictine monastery dating from 789; it was handed to the Cistercian Order in 1497 and then dissolved in 1797. The two cloisters and the assembly hall (formerly the refectory) are by Bramante; the latter contains *The Wedding at Cana*, a fresco by Callisto Piazza (16th-century).

Topping the Tempio
della Vittoria

If time allows, a quick visit to the little church of **San Bernardino** ㊱ in Via Lanzone is very rewarding; it received its present-day appearance in 1428 and the interior contains 15th-century Lombard frescoes. Not far away, in the courtyard of the house at Via Torchio 16, a section of the ancient **Roman circus** (Circo Romano) ㊲ can be seen; it used to accommodate 30,000 spectators.

Route 6

Piazza Borromeo – Ambrosiana – San Satiro

Borromeo's statue

Pointed arch portal

Go along the Via Circo (*see map, page 51*), then turn right down Via S Marta and then left a short while later along Via S Maurilio to reach the Piazza Borromeo; the old Milanese family of the Borromeo used to hold tournaments in this square. At the centre of the piazza is a copper statue (17th century, by Bussola) of San Carlo Borromeo. In 1943 the surrounding area was badly damaged during an air raid, especially the **Casa dei Borromei** ㊳, the family's palazzo, which produced Milanese cardinals Carlo Borromeo (1538–84) and Federico Borromeo (1564–1631). Today's building is a reconstruction of the former one, and use was made of as many of the original fragments (15th century) as possible. Interesting features here include the pointed-arch portal, the Lombard Gothic court of honour and the gaming hall adjoining the courtyard, which contains some very fine 15th-century frescoes.

Proceed along Via Bollo now as far as the Piazza di San Sepolcro, the site of the old Roman forum. The baths lay on the southern side of the piazza; the Palazzo Castani (18th century) was built above their foundations. Opposite the palazzo is the Church of **San Sepolcro** ㊴ (open daily 8am–6pm). Consecrated to the Holy Sepulchre in 1040, this church received its present-day appearance in the 12th and 14th century; the interior has been re-done in baroque style. A 14th-century sarcophagus in the crypt contains various relics captured by the Milanese during the Second Crusade (1147–49).

San Sepolcro

Beyond the church is the Piazza Pio XI, dominated by the ★★ **Palazzo dell'Ambrosiana** ㊵. It was built between 1603 and 1609 by Lelio Buzzi to house the library and collection of paintings that Cardinal Federico Borromeo had begun in 1595. The ground floor houses the **Biblioteca Ambrosiana** (Monday to Friday 9.30am–5pm, closed Sat-

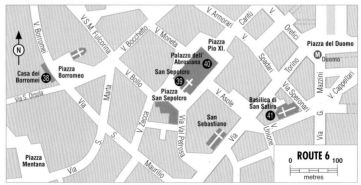

urday, Sunday and in August), which contains around 900,000 volumes and 35,000 manuscripts. The library's most valuable possessions are fragments of the *Iliad* with miniatures (5th–6th century), a book by Virgil with annotations by Petrarch, a Gothic Bible, and also the famous Codice Atlantico, a collection of drawings by Leonardo da Vinci.

Library pediment

On the upper storey is the revonated **Pinacoteca Ambrosiana** (Tuesday and Thursday 10am–5.30pm, Friday to Sunday 10am–10pm, last entry one hour prior to closing time, admission fee). This picture gallery, which has recently been extensively restored and altered, contains one of the most important collections in Milan, including many paintings of the Lombard and Venetian school. The collection of Cardinal Carlo Borromeo, which includes the masterpieces of the gallery, is displayed in rooms 1–7. The following is a list of the various rooms in the gallery detailing their main artworks:

Gallery-goers

59

I	Works by Luini, Titian, De Predis (*Portrait of a Lady*), Leonardo da Vinci (*Portrait of Beatrice d'Este*).
II	Ghirlandaio (tondo of the *Nativity*), Bergognone, Leonardo da Vinci (*Portrait of a Musician*), Botticelli (*Madonna of the Pavilion*), Pinturicchio (*Madonna with Child*), Bellini.
III	Lombard painters of the 15th and 16th century. Marco d'Oggiono, Bramantino, Luini, Salaino.
IV	Titian, Bassano (*Rest on the Flight into Egypt*).
V	Cartoon of the *School of Athens* by Raphael, Barocci, Giulio Romano.
VI	*Basket of Fruit* by Caravaggio.
VII	Flemish masters: Jan Brueghel the Elder.
VIII	Works from the 14th to 16th centuries.
IX	Italian paintings and objects from the 16th century.
X	Venetian masters of the 16th century.
XI	Italian masters of the 15th and 16th centuries. Bronzino (portrait).
XII	Venetian masters of the 16th century. Moretto, Tintoretto.
XIII	Italian and Flemish masters of the 16th and 17th centuries. Salvator Rosa, Luca Giordano, Guido Reni.
XIV	Italian masters of the 17th century.
XV	Italian masters of the 17th century. Procaccini, Crespi.
XVI	Italian masters of the 17th century. Nuvolone, Crespi.
XVII	Italian masters of the 18th century. Tiepolo, Magnasco, Fra Galgario.

San Satiro

XVIII De Pacis collection: neoclassical bronzes. Also a self-portrait by Canova.

XIX Italian masters of the 19th and early 20th century. Appiani, Hayez, Migliara, Induno, Mosè Bianchi, Previati, Gola.

XX–XXI Flemish and German masters.

The route now continues along Via Asole to Via Torino; by taking a southerly direction down this street you will come to the early baroque church of **San Sebastiano** (1577, by Pellegrino Tibaldi), and by walking north you will reach the ★ **Basilica di San Satiro ④** (Monday to Friday 8.30–11.30am, 3.30–5.30pm; note that the church is often closed for restoration, tel: 02-874683 to check before you visit).

The Cappella's ceiling

Founded in the 9th century and consecrated by Archbishop Heribert of Intimiano in 1036, San Satiro was rebuilt in Renaissance style in 1478 by Bramante. The 9th-century baptistry on Via Mazzini, which had been separate from the rest of the church until then, was incorporated by Bramante into the transept as the Cappella della Pietà, and given a Renaissance exterior. The main facade was begun by Amadeo in 1486 according to designs by Bramante, but not finally completed until 1871. The Romanesque brick campanile next to the church is also a 9th-century structure, the oldest Romanesque belltower in Lombardy.

Interior of San Satiro

San Satiro is one of the most important architectural monuments in the city. The interior is actually T-shaped, but the clever use of perspective and stucco by Bramante (false apse) makes it resemble a Greek cross; the rear wall is actually almost flat. The neoclassical high altar gains greatly from this arrangement. The much-revered votive fresco of the *Madonna and Child* (15th century) at the altar was originally outside the church; blood is said to have issued from the painting when a certain Mazzanzio da Vigolzone flung a knife at it, and since then it has been credited with miraculous powers.

Above the arches in the nave and extending into the transepts is a remarkable frieze; the coffered dome dates from 1483. The spandrels contain the *Evangelists* (16th-century) by the school of Vincenzo Foppa, a Milanese painter influenced by Bellini.

The entrance leading to the magnificent sacristy is to the right of the main portal. The coloured terracotta frieze here is by Agostino de Fondutis, and is based on designs by Bramante.

To the left of the high altar is the above-mentioned Cappella della Pietà, containing a Byzantine fresco (12th century) of *Madonna Enthroned with Child* and a polychrome terracotta *Pietà* by De Fondutis (c 1482).

Route 7

Piazza Fontana – San Nazaro Maggiore – Santa Maria
della Passione – La Rotonda

Sights 1, 2 and 3 (*see map, page 21*) have already been described in Route 2, *page 20*; (*metro Line 1, Duomo*). On
the eastern side of the Piazza Fontana stands the former
Palazzo dei Tribunali or **Palazzo del Capitano di Gio-
stizia 42**. Built between 1605 and 1750, the palazzo used
to house the city's chief magistrates. Sentences and procla-
mations were made from the balcony above the main entrance, and Milan's chief executioner resided in a room
below the roof. Later, the building was also used as a court;
it is now used by the Polizia Municipale (Vigili Urbane).

To the south, on the Piazza Santo Stefano, is the basilica of the same name (5th–11th century), and on the left
of it is the **Santuario di San Bernardino dei Monti 43**
(daily 7.30am–1pm). This octagonal church was built in
the 12th century and given its present-day baroque appearance in 1750. The covered walk in front of the building first leads to an ossuary, entirely filled with human
skulls and bones. Legend has it that these are actually
the bones of Milanese Catholics who lost their lives in the
battles with the Aryans during St Ambrose's time. In fact,
they are probably the bones brought here from the former cemetery of Santo Stefano. The skulls in the boxes
above the door are said to have been those of condemned
men. The fresco in the vault is by Sebastiano Ricci (1695).

Along the nearby Via del Perdono is the former
Ospedale Maggiore Sforzesco, now the ★ **Università
Statale 44**. The right wing of this brick building, the city's
first ever hospital, was begun in 1457 under Francesco
Sforza according to plans by Filarete, and work continued

*Details of the former Ospedale
Maggiore Sforzesco*

61

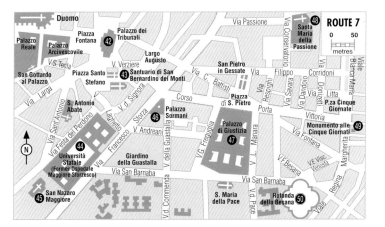

San Nazaro Maggiore

after 1465 under Guiniforte Solari and Giovanni Antonio Amadeo. The architectural style is a mixture of Gothic and Renaissance. Filarete provided the ground floor with a series of arcades on a raised plinth; the upper storey, by Solari, with its pointed-arch double windows, rests on a richly decorated cornice. The brick decor is late 15th-century Lombard; the marble busts in the spandrels of the arcades are 17th-century additions. The raised central section of the building and also the inner courtyard were built by Richini in 1624, and harmonise well with the right wing of the building which was the first part to be built. The left wing, which is not particularly interesting architecturally, was added between 1798 and 1804.

Owing to its huge dimensions (the length of the facade alone is 267m/876ft) the complex is known familiarly as Ca'Granda (The Big House). The hospital was shifted from here in 1939, and then restored after the bomb damage of 1943; today it houses Milan University's faculties of Philosophy, Letters and Law.

Students of philosophy

A silent plea

Just to the southeast is the Church of ★ **San Nazaro Maggiore ⑮** (daily 7.30am–noon and 3–6.30pm). This 4th-century church was built on the site of an Early Christian basilica, and destroyed by a fire in 1075. It is entered via the Cappella Trivulzio (1512, by Bramantino), the funeral chapel of the Trivulzio family. On the left-hand wall are valuable frescoes on either side of the altar: on the left, a *Madonna and Child with St Matronianus* (early 15th century), and on the right *Christ Appears to Mary Magdalene* (13th century). The left transept provides access to the large *Cappella di Santa Caterina* (1540) with its fine painted glass depicting scenes from the life of the saint, a German *Adoration* (16th century) and the fresco *Martyrdom of St Catherine* by Lanino (1546).

The right transept contains two Pre-Romanesque niches dating back to the original structure; the right-hand one has a *Last Supper* (16th century, by Lanino; copy of a work by Gaudenzio Ferrari), and in the left is a 15th-century bas-relief of the *Crucifixion* by Bonino da Campione.

The right transept also provides access to the sacristy, where an Early Christian silver shrine (5th century) can be admired. Beyond it is the Pre-Romanesque *Basilichetta di San Lino* (10th-century Byzantine fresco fragments).

Passing the modern clinic buildings along Via Francesco Sforza, the route now leads to the magnificent **Palazzo Sormani** . The baroque facade of this palazzo was created by Francesco Croce in 1736; the side facing the garden is neoclassical (1756, by Benedetto Alfieri). Today the palazzo houses the Biblioteca Sormani, which, with over a million volumes, is Milan's largest library. Behind the palace, in Via Francesco Sforza, are the delightful **Giardini della Guastalla** which were laid out in 1555.

Palazzo Sormani

Continue eastwards up the broad Corso di Porta Vittoria, and on the right-hand side is the enormous **Palazzo di Giustizia** . Designed according to plans by Piacentini, this monumental building, with its 120-m (394-ft) long facade, is typical of the fascistic architecture of its time (1932–40). The trapezoid ground-plan has a large courtyard of honour at its centre, 12 smaller courtyards and over 100 rooms. The courtrooms are partially decorated with sculptures, frescoes and modern mosaics.

63

Opposite the Palace of Justice is the 15th-century church of **San Pietro in Gessate** (daily 8am–6pm); it was probably built by Guiniforte Solari and was later partially renovated in baroque style.

San Pietro in Gessate
An altar of San Nazaro Maggiore

Ceiling of the Santa Maria della Passione

Part of the facade

Beyond is Via Filippo Corridoni; follow this street to the right as far as the Via Conservatorio, then turn down the latter. House No 1 here is the former monastery of the Lateran Order, and today it contains the famous Giuseppe Verdi Conservatoire and Concert hall (*see page 87*), founded in 1808. The magnificent Early Renaissance pillared courtyard, built in the first decades of the 16th century, is attributed to Cristoforo Solari. Next door is the Church of ★ **Santa Maria della Passione** ⓭ (daily 7am–noon and 3–6pm).

Construction work began on this church in 1485, and between 1511 and 1530 it was given its mighty dome by Cristoforo Solari. The nave and the baroque facade, with its reliefs depicting scenes from the Passion, date from 1692. The pillars lining the interior are decorated with paintings (1622, by Daniele Crespi) of saints and monks of the Lateran Order. The scenes from the Passion at the foot of the pilasters beneath the cupola are also by Crespi.

1 On the left, an *Entombment* fresco, 16th century.
2 *The Crown of Thorns*, a painting by Cerano; *Offertory Prayer*, by Crespi (both 16th century).
3 Fresco with the so-called *Madonna della Passione* (15th century); the painting that gave the church its name was commissioned by Archbishop Birago.
4 The *Madonna di Caravaggio*, by Bramantino.
5 Chapel of the Crucifixion with frescoes in the vault by Antonio Campi. The magnificent *Entombment* (1516) is by Bernardino Luini; the fragment of a polyptych on the right-hand wall of *Christ Between the Apostles* is attributed to Bergognone.

6 Right-hand organ (1558), with paintings by Urbini; beyond it the tomb monument of Archbishop Birago (1495, by Andrea Fusina).

7 Sacristy: on the walls and in the lunettes are frescoes by Bergognone.

8 The baroque high altar, adorned with an *Entombment* painted on an onyx slab (early 16th century) by Giulio Cesare Procaccini; the apse contains carved choir-stalls (16th century), two paintings by Lanfranco (*Resurrection* and *Ascension*), and also frescoes by Nuvolone. The vault of the apse contains a *Coronation of the Virgin*, Evangelists and sybils.

9 Left-hand organ (16th century) with paintings by Daniele Crespi.

10 The altar is decorated with a painting of the *Last Supper* (1543) by Gaudenzio Ferrari.

11 Baptistry chapel with *Last Supper of St Carlo Borromeo* (16th century) by Daniele Crespi.

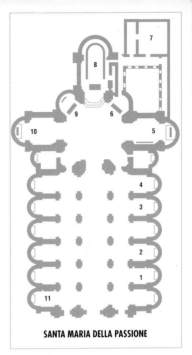

SANTA MARIA DELLA PASSIONE

After visiting this church go back to the Corso di Porta Vittoria and follow it along the left-hand side as far as the Piazzale Cinque Giornati and the **Monumento delle Cinque Giornate ㊾**. This monument, created by Giuseppe Grandi in 1895, commemorates the 'Five Days' Uprising' (between 18 and 22 March 1848). It consists of a 22-m (73-ft) high bronze obelisk bearing the names of the patriots who fell. The obelisk is surrounded by five female figures symbolising the five days, a lion and an eagle. The bell, a copy of the tower bell on the Piazza Mercanti, bears the inscription: 'Though Immobile, I Still Sound.' A crypt beneath the monument contains the bones of those who fell.

Crespi's Last Supper

Now turn right, up Viale Regina Margherita. On the corner of Via San Barnaba is the most original 18th-century building in all of Milan, the **Rotonda della Besana ㊿**. This was actually the former cemetery of the Ospedale Maggiore (*see page 61*), and was built by Francesco Raffagno between 1698 and 1725. The church, with its four wings and its octagonal central section crowned by a dome is encircled by a harmoniously laid out cloister. In 1809 Napoleon's stepson, the Viceroy of Italy, Eugène de Beauharnais, wanted to turn the building into a Pantheon of the Italian empire, but the plan could not be carried out for financial reasons. There is an open-air cinema here in the summer.

San Carlo al Corso

Route 8

Piazza del Duomo – San Carlo al Corso – Museo di Milano – Casa del Fontana – Villa Reale

This route begins at the rear of Milan Cathedral, from where the Corso Vittorio Emanuele leads on to the Piazza San Babila. The Corso used to be Milan's top fashion promenade in the 19th century, and is still one of the city's most popular thoroughfares today. Rebuilt after suffering serious bomb damage in 1943, the houses along the Corso again have their high arcades and elegant shops, ideal for shopping and strolling.

Corso mannequin

At the end of the Corso on the left and set slightly back from the street is the church of **San Carlo al Corso** 🗓. This round, neoclassical structure was built in 1838 by Carlo Amati and is consecrated to San Carlo Borromeo, cardinal of Milan. Beyond a pillared portico is the mighty dome (interior diameter 32m/106ft) plated with copper. Inside the church on the left of the entrance is a Lombard relief, *Bishop with Crib* (15th century).

The Corso now broadens out into the Piazza San Babila; the elegant Corso Matteotti also joins this square. Opposite it is the ancient **Basilica di San Babila** 🗓 (Monday to Saturday 7.30am–noon and 3.30–7pm; Sunday 7.30–1.15pm and 4.30–7pm). This restored Romanesque church was built in the 5th century on the site of a pagan temple; it was renewed in the 11th century, and then experienced several alterations. The side facades with their characteristic flying buttresses and the domed crossing with its openings for *logge* best convey the building's original ap-

San Babila fresco

pearance. The fresco and mosaic decoration in the interior is almost completely modern. An inscription inside the church states that the poet Alessandro Manzoni was baptised here on 8 August 1785. In front of the church is the Colonna del Leone (Lion's Column, 1629, by G Robecco), which according to legend was originally placed here to commemorate a Milanese victory over the Venetians.

Desirable designer

From the Piazza San Babila keen shoppers can take a detour to elegant Via Montenapoleone with its famous designer and fashion stores (Cartier, Ungaro, Gucci, Cardin, Ferragamo) and also to Via Sant'Andrea (Armani, Fendi, Hermes, Prada, Chanel, Moschino).

Also on Via Sant'Andrea, at No 6, is the **Museo di Milano** (Tuesday to Sunday 9am–1pm, 2–6pm, tel: 02-76006245, admission free). The municipal museum, housed in the 18th-century Palazzo Morando, documents the development of Milan and features a chronological exhibition of furniture, paintings, engravings, coins, medals and other items. Since 1963 the building has also housed the Museum of Contemporary History.

67

Follow Via Montenapoleone now a short way further, as far as Via Santo Spirito (Valentino, house No 3). At No 10 is the huge **Palazzo Bagatti-Valsecchi**. Built in Neo-Renaissance style in the 19th century, the palazzo contains a small art collection (Tuesday to Sunday 1–5pm; closed Monday). In the courtyard is the *Madonna del Ratt*, so named in Milanese dialect because the infant Jesus is carrying a mouse on his shoulder.

Palazzo detail

The Via S Spirito leads to the Via della Spiga (house No 4 Versace, No 23 Krizia) and the latter leads on to the Corso Venezia. The building at No 11 that housed the former priests' seminary is worth a closer look: it was built in 1564 and has a magnificent baroque portal by Richini (17th century). Opposite is the dignified ★ **Casa Fontana** , the oldest building on the Corso Venezia and generally considered to be one of the best-preserved and most typical 15th-century patrician residences in all Milan. The Casa's facade (c 1475) still retains the characteristic grace of the Lombard Renaissance and reveals the influence of Bramante. Finely worked columns shaped like candelabra adorn the main portal, and the windows have fine brick decoration.

A few steps further on the right is the enormous **Palazzo Serbelloni** . This magnificent palazzo in the city's eastern suburbs was built in 1760, but after a pause in construction it was finished in the neoclassical style by Ticino architect Simone Cantoni for the counts of Serbelloni. Napoleon Bonaparte lived here in 1796,

Palazzo del Senato

Neoclassical entrance

Gallery gathering

as did Vittorio Emanuele II in 1859. The long bas-relief frieze (by F and D Carabelli) stretching along the facade depicts the history of the Lombard League (*see page 8*). Today the palazzo is used by the Milan press club.

Further along the Corso Venezia on the right is the **Palazzo Rocca-Saporiti** (house No 40), built by Giuseppe Perego in 1812, and one of the city's finest neoclassical buildings. The sculptural decoration is by Pompeo Marchesi and Giorgio Rusca.

Taking a different street at the Palazzo Serbelloni, Via Senato leads past the church of San Pietro Celestino (1735; 14th-century campanile) and to **Palazzo del Senato** ㊿. This palace was commissioned from Fabio Mangone in 1620 by Cardinal Federico Borromeo; it was completed by Richini and initially served as a *Collegio Svizzero*, a seminary for Swiss priests. During the Napoleonic Kingdom of Italy it housed the Senate (1809–14). Today it contains the state archives.

The park opposite – English-style gardens with a small lake and a fountain (by A Wildt) – forms part of the grounds of the **Villa Reale** (Via Palestro 16). This Royal Villa was built by Viennese architect Leopold Pollak in 1790 for the counts of Barbiano di Belgioioso. The main facade, typically neoclassical, faces the park, while the entrance faces the Via Palestro and the Giardini Pubblici (*see page 41*). In 1803 the villa was purchased by the Cisalpine Republic and presented to Napoleon I, who lived here with Josephine; a stepson of Napoleon's, Eugène de Beauharnais, Viceroy of Italy, resided here too. In 1858 the Austrian field-marshal Count Joseph Radetzky died here; he had been commander-in-chief of the imperial troops in Italy from 1831 to 1857.

In 1859 the building passed into the hands of the House of Savoy, and since 1919 has been the property of the City of Milan, which installed a **Civica Galleria d'Arte Moderna** here in 1921 (Tuesday to Sunday 9.30am–5.30pm; admission free). The grand salon of the villa is of particular interest; its ceiling has a fresco of *Apollo and the Muses* by Andrea Appiani (1811).

Although the main bulk of the collection of the Galleria d'Arte Moderna has now been incorporated into the **Museo d'Arte Contemporanea** in the Palazzo Reale (*see page 20*), among the works still at the Civica Galleria are several by Marino Marini, the Vismara and Grassi collections, including art by Van Gogh, Cézanne and Corot, and also other 19th-century works (Tuesday to Sunday 9.30am–5.30pm; closed Monday, New Year's Day, Easter, 1 May, 15 August and Christmas; admission free).

A Padiglione d'Arte Contemporanea (Pavilion of Contemporary Art, 1953) stages alternating exhibitions (entrance in the courtyard, to the right of the facade).

Route 9

Piazza del Duomo – Basilica di San Lorenzo Maggiore – Archi dell'antica Porta Ticinese – Basilica di Sant'Eustorgio – Santa Maria presso San Celso

This route goes to the south of the centre. To reach the starting point from the Piazza del Duomo the best thing to do is walk down the busy Via Torino (*see map, page 21*) southwestwards as far as the long square known as the Carrobbio, and from there to take the broad Corso di Porta Ticinese southwards. On the left are the antique **Colonne di San Lorenzo**. These 16 columns once formed part of either a Roman temple or of a *thermae* complex dating from the 2nd or 3rd century AD. They were placed here in the 4th century as an entrance portico for the church beyond, the ★★ **Basilica di San Lorenzo Maggiore ⑤⑦**.

Colonne di San Lorenzo

San Lorenzo Maggiore

This church, built on Roman foundations, probably originated as an Aryan basilica in around AD 350, and only became Catholic from the time of St Ambrose onwards. The ceiling collapsed twice after conflagrations in the 11th and 12th century, and was renewed in Romanesque style. In 1573 the dome collapsed yet again and was reconstructed in Late Renaissance style by Martino Bassi.

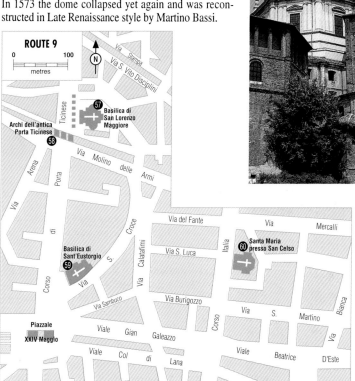

ROUTE 9

0   100
metres

Via Stampa

Via S. Vito Disciplini

Ticinese

⑤⑦ Basilica di San Lorenzo Maggiore

Archi dell'antica Porta Ticinese ⑤⑧

Via Molino delle Armi

Arena

Porta

Via di

Croce

S. Calatafimi

Via del Fante

Via S. Luca

Via

Italia

Mercalli

⑥⓪ Santa Maria presso San Celso

Basilica di Sant'Eustorgio ⑤⑨

Via S.

Via Sambuco

Via Burigozzo

Corso

Via S. Martino

Bianca

Via

Piazzale XXIV Maggio

Viale Gian Galeazzo

Corso

Viale Beatrice D'Este

Viale Col di Lana

Constantine

In front of the modern facade (1894, by Cesare Nova) stands a bronze copy of a statue of Constantine, commemorating the Milan Edict of Tolerance (313).

The octagonal interior, surrounded by a covered walk, has been extended on the four main sides by large semi-spherical exedrae; these are two storeys in height and are supported alternately by four round and four octagonal pillars. The baroque main altar has a fresco of the *Madonna and Child* that was originally outside the building; beyond the high altar is the Cappella di Sant'Ippolito with four antique marble columns, dating to the 4th century. On the left of the high altar is the tomb of Giovanni del Conte, by Marco d'Agrate and Vincenzo Seregni (16th century); on the right is the tomb of the Robbiano family with a *Madonna with Saints* fresco (both 1411). Next to this tomb is the entrance to the Cappella Cittadini, formerly Romanesque and then renovated in Gothic style in the 15th century, with remains of some 13th-century frescoes.

The Cappella di Sant'Aquilino is of particular interest. From the middle of the basilica, turn right through a portal (with an 11th-century *Entombment* fresco on the left) and enter a square atrium containing mosaic fragments from the 4th century, and also a 14th-century *Crucifixion* fresco. A Roman portal (3rd century, with depictions of circus games) then leads to an octagonal chapel dating from the 4th century and originally built as a baptistry. The two niches at the back contain 4th-century Roman-Christian mosaics depicting *Christ Among the Apostles* and *The Abduction of Elijah*. Opposite the entrance is a silver sarcophagus (16th century, by C Garavaglia) containing the mortal remains of St Aquilinius; next to it, a flight of steps leads to the subterranean remains of an earlier Roman building (2nd century BC). On the right of the tomb of St Aquilinius is a 5th-century marble sarcophagus, which according to legend was built for Galla Placidia, daughter of the emperor Theodosius. A further flight of steps leads to the centre section of the basilica, decorated with 4th- and 5th-century frescoes.

Opposite the Cappella di Sant'Aquilino is the 15th-century Cappella di San Sisto; the fresco decoration here dates from the 17th century.

Time for lunch

Porta Ticinese

The route now continues along the Corso di Porta Ticinese, passing the **Archi dell'antica Porta Ticinese** ⑤⑧, a lively, bohemian district. The arches of this old city gate formed part of the city wall erected in 1171 after the destruction of Milan by Barbarossa. Traditionally, all the important people in the city would enter by this gate; even today, newly elected archbishops take this route. On the outside is a relief (c 1330) by the Pisan artist Giovanni di Balduccio. It portrays the *Madonna and Saints, with St Ambrose Handing Over the Model of the City*.

Follow the Corso di Porta Ticinese further southwards; at the end on the left is the little Piazza Sant'Eustorgio, at the centre of which is the statue *St Peter Martyr* (c 1680). Beyond it is the recently restored **Basilica di Sant'Eustorgio** ⑤⑨ (daily 7.30am–noon, 3.30–6.30pm). It was built in in the 11th century on the site of an oratory, founded by Bishop Eustorgius before 400 and according to legend contained the relics of the Three Magi, presented to the bishop by the Emperor Constantine. In 1227 the church became the property of the Dominican Order; they made it Gothic in 1278, and after several alterations and additions it was given a baroque appearance in the 17th century. In 1862 the medieval structure of the building was again emphasised, by Giovanni Brocca. An open-air stone pulpit, erected in 1597, stands on the left-hand corner of the facade; it replaced the former wooden one from which St Peter Martyr preached against the heretics.

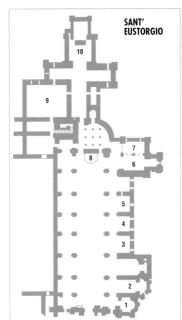

SANT' EUSTORGIO

71

The large pillars (12th century), which are decorated with carvings of fabulous creatures, stand out in the gloom of the three-aisled interior.

1 Cappella dei Brivio (1484, renewed in the 19th century) with the superb tomb monument to Giacomo S Brivio (by Tommaso Cazzaniga).

2 The Cappella dei Torelli, built in 1424; contains the tomb monument of Pietro Torelli by Jacopino da Tradate (1416).

3 Cappella dei Visconti (14th century), with wall and ceiling frescoes dating from when the church was built. Mausoleum of Stefano Visconti (died 1327) and his wife, a work by Pisan artist Giovanni di Balduccio, and Bonino da Campione. Below the frescoes, a painted wooden crucifix (Venetian school, 15th century).

4 At the altar, a *Madonna, Child and Saints* (late 16th century, attributed to Cerano).

5 Cappella Visconti (younger branch of the family) containing various tombs. The clothing on the recumbent statue on the tomb-slab of Agnese Besozzi (1417, by Jacopino da Tradate) is of particular interest.

6 In the right transept are two 14th-century sarcophagi; above them the *Adoration of the Magi* (15th century).

7 Cappella dei Magi (Chapel of the Wise Men). The large Roman sarcophagus held the relics of the Three Magi until 1164 (they are now in Cologne). Above the altar is some fine 14th-century sculpture.

Sant' Eustorgio

Wrought ironwork

8 The large marble panel on the high altar (14th century) with its scenes from the passion is considered the finest marble work of this period in Milan. The high altar houses the remains of St Eustorgius.

9 Sacristy (1575) with magnificent baroque cabinets.

10 The Cappella Portinari, one of the greatest examples of Renaissance art in Milan, was created by the Florentine artist Michelozzo Michelozzi between 1462 and 1466. The chapel was commissioned by the banker Pigello Portinari, who founded it to house the relics of St Peter Martyr and as his own resting place. At the centre of the chapel stands the saint's sarcophagus, the magnificent Arca di San Pietro Martire (1335–39) made of Carrara marble, a masterpiece by the Pisan artist Giovanni di Balduccio. The sarcophagus, decorated with scenes from the life of the saint, is supported by eight pillars with allegorical statues of the Virtues that are extraordinarily graceful. Above the sarcophagus is a tabernacle with the statue of the *Madonna Between St Dominic and St Peter Martyr.* The silver reliquary in a small chapel to the left of the altar contains the skull of the saint. The frieze decorating the chapel, with its fine angels' heads (late 15th century, possibly by Amadeo) is enchanting. The wall paintings depicting scenes from the life of the saint, as well as an *Annunciation* and an *Assumption,* date from the 15th century and are probably by Vincenzo Foppa.

Arca di San Pietro Martire

Santa Maria presso San Celso

Next to the church, on the Piazza XXIV Maggio, lies the Porta Ticinese (c 1800) and to the west of it, Milan's old harbour basin *(Darsena),* now the gateway to the heart of Milanese nightlife *(see page 87).* Turn eastwards now and take the Via Sambuco and Via Burigozzo as far as the Corso Italia, and the church of ★ **Santa Maria presso San Celso** ⑥⓪ (daily 8.30am–noon and 4–5.30pm).

It was begun in 1493 according to plans by Giovanni Dolcebuono, and then continued by Cristoforo Solari and Giovanni Antonio Amadeo. In 1513 it was given its Bramante-style atrium by Cesariano, and the facade – a masterpiece of Renaissance architecture – was added by Galeazzo Alessi between 1569 and 1572.

The interior, also by Alessi, contains a series of magnificent 16th-century paintings: at the altar in the right transept is a *Holy Family* by Paris Bordone; the central chapel in the ambulatory contains a *Baptism of Christ* by Gaudenzio Ferrari; and at the left-hand end of the ambulatory is a *Confession of St Paul* by Moretto. In the altar of the left transept is an Early Christian sarcophagus (5th century) with biblical scenes. The neighbouring sacristy contains fine gold items. Opposite the sacristy is the entrance to the 10th-century church of San Celso.

Ceiling decoration

Additional Sights

Here are a few more sights not included in the nine routes so far described.

Piazza Duca d'Aosta. This square is the centre of modern Milan. The monumental main station (Stazione Centrale, Metro lines M2 and M3) on this square is one of the largest in Europe. Designed by Ulisse Stacchini in 1906, it was finally built between 1926 and 1934.

One of the landmarks of modern Milan is the huge skyscraper opposite the station, the **Pirelli Building**, designed by architects Ponti, Fornaroli, Roselli, Dell'Orto and Nervi. Built between 1955 and 1959, and 127m (417ft) high, it is one of the tallest concrete structures in the world.

On a pedestal at the Fiera Milano

Fiera Milano. The Great Milanese Fair (*Metro M1, Amendola Fiera*) first took place in 1920 on the bastions near the Porta Venezia, and was shifted to its present location on the site of an old parade ground in 1923. Today's Milan Fair is not just one fair, but dozens of fairs taking place one after the other right through the year and representing a huge variety of trades and interests, from wine-growing to telecommunications, fashion to sanitary ware, antiques to cartoons and tourism to the environment. The exhibition halls cover a vast area and space has been further increased by the addition of the Portello buildings. One architecturally notable building is the machine pavilion designed by the architect Nervi, with its 'fan' roof.

73

★ **Certosa di Garegnano** (on the northwest outskirts; *tram No 14 from Via Orefici*). Also known as Certosa di Milano, this Carthusian monastery can be reached along Viale Certosa and Via Garegnano. Founded by Archbishop Giovanni Visconti in 1349, the monastery was replaced by the present structure between 1562 and 1570 by Vin-

Stazione Centrale

Abbazia di Chiaravalle

The abbey walls

Fishing on Lake Idroscalo

cenzo Seregni. Inside the monastery church, along the walls in the nave, there is a very dramatic fresco cycle by Daniele Crespi (1628–9) illustrating the history of the Order and the life of its founder, St Bruno.

★ **Abbazia di Chiaravalle** (on the southeastern outskirts of the city; *tram No 13 from Piazza del Duomo*; open Tuesday to Sunday 9–noon and 2–5pm). This abbey, which can be reached via the Corso di Porta Romana, the Piazzale Corvetto and the Via Polesine, was founded as the first Cistercian abbey in Italy in 1135 by St Bernard of Clairvaux. Its celebrated Romanesque Gothic brick church, consecrated in 1221, has a square tower that can be seen for miles around, and is made up of several galleries with numerous storeys.

Particular highlights inside the church include frescoes in the dome (15th-century Milan school), the choir-stalls (1465) and also a fresco of the *Madonna* (1523) by Bernardino Luini on the upper landing in the right transept. The sacristy contains the 16th-century *Holy Family* altarpiece of the Leonardo da Vinci school. The right transept leads to a delightful 13th-century Gothic cloister; the small square campanile dates from 1568.

Idroscalo (to the east of the city). Situated next to Linate Airport, the *Idroscalo* can be reached along the Via Forlanini; it was created between 1928 and 1937. The basin is 2.5km (2 miles) long, 300m (980ft) wide and almost 3m (10ft) deep. The water comes from a crevasse, and is diverted into the River Lambro along a canal. The Idroscalo is also referred to as the Riviera di Milano because an elegant bathing resort has sprung up on its shores. Motor-boat races and rowing contests are held here on a regular basis, as is a summer festival.

Excursions

Milan is the ideal starting-point for brief as well as lengthy excursions into the surrounding area (train links from the Stazione Centrale with Monza, Pavia and Bergamo, and from the Stazione Nord with the Northern Italian lakes).

Monza

During medieval times this small town, roughly 15km (9 miles) to the northwest of Milan (162m/530ft above sea level; population 122,476) was where the Lombard kings were crowned (information: Piazza Carducci). The main architectural highlight is the 14th-century ★ **Duomo di San Giovanni**, built by Matteo da Campione in the Lombard Gothic style on the site of a church founded by Lombard Queen Theodolinda. The relief above the main portal depicting the queen, her husband Authari and the Baptism of Christ, came from the previous building on this site. To the left of the choir in this five-aisled basilica is the ★ Cappella della Regina Teodolinda; on the altar, inside a crucifix, is the Iron Crown of the Lombards (9th century). The crown is a headband of beaten gold, studded with precious stones and with an iron rim that is said to have been made from one of the nails of the True Cross. Thirty-four Lombard monarchs were crowned with it, most recently

Duomo di San Giovanni

The Iron Crown

75

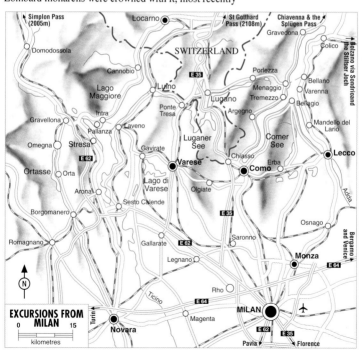

EXCURSIONS FROM MILAN
0   15
kilometres

Charles V (1530), Napoleon (1805) and Ferdinand I of Austria (1836). (Conducted tours. Information from the Museo del Duomo.) The left transept leads on to the Museo del Duomo, where the cathedral treasure can be admired.

Arengario: This old, restored communal palace was originally built in 1293; the top of the tower, with the Ghibelline battlements, dates from the 14th century.

★★ **Parco di Monza**. This 800-ha (1,977-acre) park extends to the north of the town. The southern part of it contains the neoclassical ★ **Villa Reale** (1776–80, by Giuseppe Piermarini), also known as The Versailles of Lombardy. The north wing of the castle contains a collection of 19th-century paintings. The section of park behind the castle has been laid out very romantically (a lake, grottoes). The park (bicycle hire at the entrance on Viale Cavriga; also golf, tennis and pool), through which the River Lambro flows, extends a long way northwards, as far as the *Autodromo*, where national and international motor-racing events are held regularly.

The Villa Reale

Northern Italian Lakes

The route described here roughly follows the one usually taken on organised day trips (*see page 98*). The Swiss canton of Ticino extends between Lake Maggiore and Lake Como.

The shortest connection between Milan and Lake Maggiore is via the Autostrada dei Laghi, which leads to Sesto Calende (54km/34 miles). Lake Maggiore is 212sq km (82sq miles) in size, about 65km (40 miles) long, 5km (3 miles) wide and 372m (1,200ft) deep and the largest lake in Italy after Lake Garda. The Ticino river flows through it. Its northern end is part of Switzerland. The journey now continues along the western bank of the lake as far as:

Fountain in Stresa

★ **Stresa** (210m/688ft above sea-level; population 5,000). Situated 79km (49 miles) from Milan, Stresa is one of the most elegant tourist destinations on Lake Maggiore (information from APT, Piazzale Europa, tel: 0323-30150). From here take an excursion to Monte Mottarone (1,491m/4,890ft; cable-car), which also has a good road leading up it; at the top is a superb view across the Alps.

Isola dei Pescatori

Another highly recommended trip is to take a motorboat from Stresa to the ★★ **Borromean Islands**. This group of islands consists of the Isola dei Pescatori (Fishermen's Island), the Isola Madre (Mother Island), the tiny island of San Giovanni and the much-praised Isola Bella (Beautiful Island); this last island has the magnificent baroque castle belonging to the counts of Borromeo (1650–71; tapestries, paintings, porcelain, weapons collection and an 18th-century puppet theatre), and ten garden terraces with a delightful mix of subtropical flora and rare white peacocks.

Beyond Stresa the route passes through Gravellona (91km/56 miles), where you can make a rewarding detour to tiny **Lake Orta** (6km/4 miles) with its idyllic island of San Giulio. The route continues on round the Bay of Pallanza towards **Pallanza**, an elegant health spa on a sheltered site, before reaching Intra (ferry connection from here to Locarno). From here, take the car ferry to Laveno.

On Lake Maggiore

We now leave Lake Maggiore and travel to Gavirate (118km/73 miles) from where there's a superb view across the Lago di Varese.

Varese (382m/1,253ft above sea-level; population 84,000), 130km (81) miles from Milan, is a popular excursion destination for the Milanese (information from APT, Via Ippodromo 9, tel: 0332-284624). The Church of San Vittore is definitely worth a visit; it was built by Giuseppe Bernascone between 1580 and 1615 according to designs by Pellegrino Tibaldi. The 72-m (236-ft) high campanile was built in the 17th–18th century. Beyond the church is a 12th-century Romanesque baptistry. A walk through the Giardini Pubblici (Villa Mirabello) is quite delightful. Rewarding excursion destinations near here include the Sacro Monte (880m/2,880ft) and the Campo dei Fiori (1,226m/4,022ft); both have great views.

San Vittore

77

The route now leaves Varese and continues via Olgiate as far as Lake Como (Lago di Como). This lake (150sq km/ 58sq miles, 50km/30 miles long and 4.5km/ 2¾ miles wide) is the deepest inland lake in Europe at 410m (1,345ft), and is enclosed by mountains between 1,500m (4,900ft) and 2,100m (6,890ft) in height. Villas and gardens line its banks. The southern part divides into a western and an eastern half (Lago di Lecco).

★ **Como** (202m/663ft above sea-level; population 93,000), 156km (97 miles) from Milan, is a centre of the silk industry and a holiday town (information from APT, Piazza Cavour 17, tel: 031-3300111). An important sight here is the cathedral, which began as a Gothic one in 1396 and was then completed, predominantly in Renaissance style, in around 1600. The Turin architect Juvara finally completed the cathedral in the 18th century when he added the 75-m (246-ft) high dome. Other highlights of the town include the Broletto (Old Town Hall, built in 1215); the Porta Vittoria in the city wall containing remains of the 2nd-century Porta Romana; the 11th-century Church of Sant'Abbondio, a fine example of the Lombard Romanesque style; and the Basilica San Fedele (12th century, with 11th-century portal sculpture).

Como Cathedral

On the edge of the lake in the Giardino Pubblico is the Mausoleo Voltiano (Voltiano temple), erected to commemorate the physicist Alessandro Volta, who was born here (1745–1827) and after whom the electrical unit volt is named.

On the promenade at Como

A walk along the promenade is very rewarding, as is an excursion to Brunate (716m/2,349ft), with its magnificent view out across the lake.

Continuing now along the western bank of Lake Como, the route travels via Argegno, Tremezzo (186km/116 miles; Mussolini was shot dead not far from the nearby village of Mezzegra, on 27 April 1945) and finally just before Cadenabbia (187km/116 miles) it reaches the magnificent Villa Carlotta (1747) with its splendid garden.

Menaggio (203m/666ft above sea-level; population around 4,500), 191km (120 miles) from Milan, is a picturesque and much-visited little town built on a promontory (information: Via Lusardi 8), and is the starting-point for an excursion to Loveno sopra Menaggio (about 1.5km/1 mile), from where there is a spectacular view of Bellagio at the tip of the peninsula.

Via Gravedona (199km/118 miles from Milan) and Colico (216km/134 miles from Milan) – or via the car ferry from Menaggio – we now reach ★ **Varenna** (220m/720ft above sea-level; population 4,500), 240km (150) miles from Milan, a picturesquely situated town on the east bank. The extremely narrow streets fall steeply down to the lake. Above the town (346m/1,135ft) is the ruin of the Castello di Vezio. There are car ferry connections from here to Bellagi, where there are some fine gardens and villas.

Lecco

Lecco (214m/700ft above sea-level; population 46,000), 266km (165 miles), an industrial and commercial centre, is also a popular excursion destination (information from Via Nazario Sauro 6). The remains of the 14th-century fortifications are fascinating, and a visit to the Duomo and the Palazzo del Caleotto – where Alessandro Manzoni used to live – is rewarding. Lecco is the starting-point for trips up to the Pizzo d'Erna (1,373m/4,500ft) and Monte Coltignone (1,774m/5,820ft).

From Lecco, Milan can be regained via the *superstrada* motorway (316km/196 miles).

Bergamo

Bergamo (249m/817ft above sea-level; population around 108,000), 51km (31 miles) to the east of Milan along the Autostrada Serenissima, was an important trading centre as far back as Roman times. It consists of two distinct halves: the medieval Upper Town, lying on a hill and enclosed by a Venetian wall (Bergamo Alta) and the modern Lower Town (Bergamo Bassa) with the busy Piazza Vittorio Veneto at its centre. The Teatro Donizetti, named after the opera composer who was born in the town, is also here. There is a monument to him on the Piazza Cavour, next to the theatre (information from APT, Via Papa Giovanni 106, tel: 035-211020 and Vicolo Aquila Nera). Definitely worth a visit in the Lower Town is the Pinacoteca dell' Accademia Carrara; the gallery contains a superb collection by Bergamo artists (Ghislandi, Bascheni), other Italian artists (Botticelli, Raphael, Tintoretto) and international masters (Cranach, Dürer, Rubens, Van Dyck).

The first place to visit in the picturesque Upper Town – which can also be reached along Viale Vittorio Emanuele via a funicular railway – is the Palazzo della Ragione (12th century) on the Piazza Vecchia. This is the oldest town hall in Italy.

Very close by are the Piazza del Duomo, with the cathedral of Sant'Alessandro (15th–17th century; facade and dome are modern additions), the Church of Santa Maria Maggiore (12th–14th century; baroque interior) with its ★ **Cappella Colleoni**. This magnificent Renaissance chapel was built between 1470 and 1475 as a mausoleum for the Venetian *condottiere* Bartolomeo Colleoni. Its unusually ornate marble facade is decorated with medallions. The chapel's interior, decorated with frescoes by Tiepolo (18th century) contains the tombs of the military leader Colleoni and his daughter Meda.

In the Cappella Colleoni

There is a superb view across the city from up on the Rocca, Bergamo's citadel, built in the 14th century.

★★ Certosa di Pavia

Open Tuesday to Sunday 9–11.30am and 2.30–4.30pm, (6pm in summer, 4pm in winter); closed Monday. A monk conducts tours of the building; a small tip is expected.

This former Carthusian monastery, situated roughly 27km (17 miles) to the south of Milan, can be reached along the N35 which follows the course of the Naviglio Pavese; turn off it 9km/6 miles beyond Binasco (Filippo

On the road to Certosa

Certosa di Pavia

Above the High Altar

Maria Visconti had his wife Beatrice murdered in the castle here in 1418). The monastery was founded in 1396 by Gian Galeazzo Visconti and is one of the most important architectural and cultural monuments in Italy. It was originally designed as a mausoleum for the Visconti family. The first architect was Bernardo da Venezia; he was followed by Cristoforo da Cingo and Giacomo da Campione. In 1420 Giovanni Solari also worked here, and his son Guiniforte in 1453. The magnificent, almost over-ornate facade (15th century) is by Giovanni Antonio Amadeo; he was assisted by Milanese goldsmith-sculptors Cristoforo and Antonio Mantegazza between 1464 and 1495. It is considered to be the finest example of the Lombard style in existence. In the 16th century the building was finally completed in the Renaissance style.

The monastery contains several superb pieces of sculpture, impressive wood carvings, bronzes and wrought-iron grilles, marble mosaics, intarsias, colourful stained-glass windows and several very valuable paintings. Highlights inside the building include the tomb of Lodovico il Moro and his wife Beatrice d'Este in the left transept, a work by Cristoforo Solari (1498). The second chapel in the left side-aisle contains a 15th-century polyptych by Perugino and Bergognone. The triptych made of hippopotamus tusk with 66 bas-reliefs and 94 statuettes, and on display in the old sacristy, is from the workshop of Baldassare degli Embriachi and is Venetian (1400–9). Also of interest in the monastery are the high altar, the 15th-century choir-stalls, and the ceiling decoration in the 'new' sacristy by Pietro Solari (1600). In the right transept also note the entrance-gate to the Fountain Chapel with the busts of the seven duchesses of Milan (15th century).

The Little Cloister is a pleasant, covered walkway with delightful terracotta decoration (c 1465); it was built by

Rinaldo de Stauris from Cremona. The 122 arches of the Great Cloister are supported by marble columns; the 24 little rooms belonging to the monks seem rather too cosy, and no longer resemble proper cells. Francois I of France was was held captive in the rooms adjoining the Great Cloister after the Battle of Pavia in 1525.

Pavia

This small town on the Ticino river, 36km (22 miles) south of Milan and around 10km (6 miles) to the south of the Certosa (77m/250ft above sea-level; population 100,000), has a sort of gloomy magnificence about it. Formerly a Roman settlement, it was later one of the last bastions of the Goths, then a Byzantine fortress, and finally capital of the Lombard Kingdom, remaining so until the 11th century. Pavia actually eclipsed Milan in its importance. Under the Visconti the town became the intellectual and artistic centre of Lombardy, and rivals Bologna as home of the oldest university in Italy (information from APT, Via Fabio Filzi 2, tel: 0382-27238).

The many patricians' houses and palazzi around the Piazza Municipio in the eastern part of the town also testify to its cultural heritage.

The Duomo (1488–1609) is considered the finest example of Lombard Renaissance architecture in Italy. Bramante, Leonardo da Vinci and Giovanni Amadeo are just a few of the artists who worked on it. The site was originally occupied by two churches, Santo Stefano and Santa Maria del Popolo; fragments of the former can still be seen next to the ruins of the old Torre Civica that was once attached to the Duomo. This tower, the base of which dates back to the 11th century, collapsed on 17 March 1989, for reasons that are still unclear. The cathedral is the burial place of San Siro, Pavia's first bishop. Its magnificent dome, only completed in 1885, is the third largest in Italy and is the symbol of the town.

The nearby Basilica of San Michele, where emperors and kings were crowned during the Middle Ages (including Barbarossa in 1155) is Pavia's oldest Romanesque church. It was founded in 661 and was given its present-day appearance in the 12th century. Real highlights here are the facade with its magnificent sculpture decoration, and the huge Romanesque mosaic above the presbytery.

Another important Romanesque building is San Pietro in Ciel d'Oro; its (formerly gold) ceiling gets a mention in Dante's *Divine Comedy*. Lombard king Luitprand had the bones of St Augustine buried here in the year 725.

North of the town is the still-mighty Castello dei Visconti (14th century), now home to the municipal musuem; to the south is the Ponte Vecchio, a covered bridge across the Ticino river (1354, restored) is also worth a detour.

Pavia's coat-of-arms

81

The Duomo

Art History

Opposite: Bronze door, Milan Cathedral

Architecture

There are few visible remains in Milan that date back to Roman times, the most notable examples being the ruins of a huge Roman circus and the remains of Colonne di San Lorenzo, columns of a building dating back to the 2nd or 3rd century AD. As far as vestiges of the Early Christian era are concerned, the squat architectural style of the 4th century is clearly visible in the church of San Lorenzo.

Colonne di San Lorenzo

We come across the Romanesque in a number of sacred buildings. On the one hand (more so than in the rest of Italy) these buildings reflect traditional styles; on the other hand, they show a marked similarity with South German architecture of the same period – during the 11th and 12th century Lombardy was the focus of German interests in the south. Dark but clearly proportioned churches with richly decorated portals and porches, as well as square bell towers on the facades are especially characteristic of the Lombard Romanesque style, the most important exponents of which were master builders from Como (Maestri Comacini). The oldest churches of this type in Milan are San Celso (10th century) and San Babila (11th century), while Sant'Ambrogio (11–12th century) and San Simpliciano (12th century) are considered to be the most stylistically pure. San Michele and San Pietro in Ciel d'Oro (12th century) in Pavia, both Sant'Abbondio (11th century) and San Fedele (12th century) in Como, and Bergamo's basilica of Santa Maria Maggiore (12th century) also date back to this era.

Sant'Ambrogio

Originally created in France, the Gothic style was first established in Lombardy in the mid-13th century. While the Italian Gothic adopts the French innovation of the pointed arch, it generally leaves out the flying buttresses, maintaining the solid walls so typical of the Romanesque. The Lombard builders were not keen on the upwards-striving style of the Gothic, instead preferring classical horizontal lines and broad interior spaces. Even Milan Cathedral (begun 1386), which could be said to be the most strongly Gothic church in Italy and certainly recalls the French style in many of its features, also evinces a great deal of influence from the Northern Italian tradition. In other Gothic churches of Milan, too, such as San Marco (1254), San Gottardo (1336) and the Abbey of Chiaravalle (12th and 13th century), the Lombard rearrangement of the Gothic is plainly evident, as indeed it is in the magnificent Gothic cathedral of Como, which was built between the 14th–16th century.

San Marco

Florentine builders began to replace the Gothic style c 1400 by initiating a rebirth of classical motifs and features. Rounded arches, classical columns and great em-

Ospedale Maggiore

Inside Santa Maria delle Grazie

phasis on the horizontal, achieved for example by cornices, are all characteristic components of the Renaissance style in architecture.

However, it wasn't until 1456 that the Early Renaissance arrived as far north as Milan: despite fierce resistance from the Lombard artists and architects who wanted to retain the pointed arch, the Florentine Antonio Averulino, known as Filarete, built the former Ospedale Maggiore and the gate tower of the Castello Sforzesco. The Renaissance in Milan achieved its final breakthrough with the Portinari Chapel in the Church of Sant' Eustorgio, the work of another Florentine, Michelozzo Michelozzi (1396–1472), a pupil of Donatello.

The climax of Renaissance architecture in Milan is represented in the creations of Donato Bramante (1444–1514) from Urbino, who worked in the city for Lodovico il Moro from 1480 to 1499 and produced the choir and dome of Santa Maria delle Grazie and the baptistry of Santa Maria presso San Satiro. Bramante succeeded in endowing Lombard brickwork with decorative splendour and incredible delicacy at the same time.

Bramante's influence is also evident in the buildings of the architect family Solari, especially Cristoforo Solari (called Il Gobbo, died 1525). Aside from these, Giovanni Antonio Amadeo (1447–1522) from Pavia emerged as the most important Lombard Renaissance architect, designing the facade of the Carthusian monastery in Pavia and the Colleoni Chapel in Bergamo.

The greatest exponent of the Late Renaissance in Milan is the Perugian Galeazzo Alessi (1512–72), who designed the Palazzo Marino, while the works of the Bolognese master Pellegrino Tibaldi (1532–96) in the courtyard of the archbishop's palace, already mark a transition to early baroque.

Of the baroque masters of the 17th century, Lorenzo Binaghi (facade of Sant' Alessandro) and Francesco Maria Richini (Palazzo Brera and parts of the former Ospedale Maggiore) are the most notable. Exponents of neoclassicism include Giuseppe Piermarini (1734–1808) with numerous buildings including the world-famous Teatro alla Scala and the Palazzo Reale, while perhaps the greatest building of the 19th century in Milan is the magnificent Galleria Vittorio Emanuele designed by Giuseppe Mengoni. Among the numerous modern buildings in the city, the skyscraper of the firm Pirelli (1955–9) succeeds in making a most striking impression.

Galleria Vittorio Emanuele

Sculpture

Developments in Lombard sculpture were slow, lagging behind the rest of Italy until well into the 14th century. The first major impulses were provided by the great tomb sculptures of Giovanni di Balduccio, who had arrived in Milan from Pisa and worked here with his students betwenn 1321 and 1339.

However, it was the influence of Tuscan Renaissance that led to the blossoming c 1460 of a Lombard sculptural school that was soon to have an enormous impact on developments throughout Italy. The principal exponents of the art were Cristoforo Mantegazza (died 1482), Giovanni Antonio Amadeo (who was also an architect), Cristoforo Solari and Tommaso Rodari (1487–1533). High Renaissance masters included Cristoforo Foppa (called Caradosso, 1445–1527) who was also a renowned goldsmith, and Agostino Busti (called Bambaia, 1480–1548), whose works mark the completion of the development of Lombard sculpture.

Balduccio's sculpted figures

85

Painting

Heading the list of Lombard painters is Vincenzo Foppa (died 1515), who was trained in Padua and displayed a strongly traditional approach. Foppa was followed by his poetically inclined student Ambrogio da Fossano, called Borgognone (died 1523). Influenced initially by Vincenzo Foppa and then by Bramante, the Milanese Bartolomeo Suardi, called Bramantino (1455–1536), possessed a changing sense of style.

The high point of Renaissance painting in Milan is undoubtedly marked by the works of the great master Leonardo da Vinci (1452–1519), who lived and worked in Milan between 1482–1500 and 1506–8. With his use of light and shade and his mastery of dramatic composition, it was Leonardo who set the standards for future painting. His recently restored *Last Supper* fresco in the church of Santa Maria delle Grazie is indeed one of the world's great masterpieces.

Leonardo's Last Supper

Boltraffio portrait

Among Leonardo's closest students were Giovanni Boltraffio (1467–1516), Marco D'Oggionó (1470–1530), Cesare da Sesto (died in 1521), Andrea Salaino (1470–1515) and Giampietrino (active from 1508–21), but Bernardino Luini (1470–1530) was the most lauded of his successors. Gaudenzio Ferrari (1471–1546) and his student Bernardino Lanino (died 1578) are two of the finest Lombard Renaissance painters. The principal exponent of neoclassicism is Andrea Appiani (1754–1817), while the 19th century is best represented by the works of Francesco Hayez (1754–1815), for example *The Kiss* of 1859.

Literature and music

One of the most important Italian poets of the 18th century was the Milan resident Giuseppe Parini (1729–99), whose elegant satires were later taken up by Carlo Porta (1775–1821) in his dialect poetry. Among the 19th-century Romantics, the Milanese Alessandro Manzoni (1785–1873) is famous for his historical novels such as *The Betrothed*, a Milanese novel of the 17th century.

Statue of Manzoni

Of immense importance for the development of European music as a whole was the introduction of hymns in church by the Milanese archbishop St Ambrose (339–397). In more recent times the development of opera has been closely linked with the Teatro alla Scala. Bergamo-born Gaetano Donizetti (1797–1848) and Giuseppe Verdi (1813–1901) and Umberto Giordano (1867–1948) are just some of the internationally known local names associated with operatic life in Milan. Just as immortal is the name of the star conductor of the Scala, Arturo Toscanini (1867–1957), as well as Maurizio Pollini, Claudio Abbado and Riccardo Chailly.

Music, Theatre and Nightlife

Opera and concerts

Famed for its superb opera performances and its wonderful acoustics, the **Teatro alla Scala's** opera season runs from 7 December (the day of Milan's patron saint Sant'Ambrogio) until the end of May. A programme of concerts runs from June to mid-July and from October until November. La Scale also shows ballet in September. To attend a performance at La Scala, book through the box-office on the left-hand side of the opera house or call La Scala Infotel on 02-72003744 (English spoken). You can also book via the web at www.lascala.milano.it or through the La Prevendità reservation service at Virgin Megastore, Piazza Duomo, tel: 02-72003370.

Ballet in action

The majority of other concerts are held in churches. Main venues include: the **Chiesa di S Marco** (Piazza S Marco 2) for religious music; the **Civica Scuola di Musica** (Via Stilicone 36) for more contemporary music; the **Conservatorio Giuseppe Verdi** (Via Conservatorio 12), a former monastery that puts on concerts by various orchestras almost daily; the **Musica e Poesia a S Maurizio** (Church of S Maurizio on the Corso Magenta) for ancient and baroque music; the **Chiesa di Santa Maria del Carmine** (Piazza del Carmine 2) that stages regular concerts, from chamber music to Gregorian chant; and **Teatro delle Erbe** (Via Mercato 3) for classical and guitar works. Rock music concerts take place at **Palavobis** (M1, Lampugnano) or at **Filaforum di Assago** (M2 Romolo and shuttle bus).

87

Theatre

In comparison to other large cities in Italy, Milan has a lively theatre scene with numerous permanent theatres and independent groups. If you think your knowledge of the Italian language is too rudimentary to follow a major performance, you might still enjoy a visit to the **Piccolo Teatro di Milano** founded by Giorgio Strehler (Via Rovello 2) and the **Nuovo Piccolo Teatro** (Largo Greppi). **Teatro Franco Parenti** (Via Pier Lombardo 14) stages plays and concerts, including musicals for children.

The navigli quarter at night

Nightlife

The brochure *Milano Mese*, available from the tourist office, includes listings of what's on where. Although there is too little space here to give individual listings of night spots such as bars, cabarets, piano bars and discos, good areas to visit at night include the Brera, where you can watch many a stylish Milanese taking an evening stroll, and the increasingly fashionable canal *(navigli)* area in the southwest of the city. If you fancy an evening at the cinema, many of Milan's big screens are on the Corso Vittorio Emanuele.

Food and Drink

Strictly speaking, Italian cuisine as such doesn't actually exist; instead there are a host of regional variations. Luckily, in Milan it is possible to sample not only the local Milanese specialities but those from elsewhere in the country as well (*see restaurant recommendations, page 90*). Although Milan is an expensive city, food prices are very reasonable and you can eat out very well here on a modest budget.

If you don't want to have breakfast at your hotel, you can go out to one of the many cafes or bars in Milan to breakfast instead. A day can start with an *espresso* coffee, dark and very strong, or less strong (*caffè lungo*) or a *cappuccino*, and, of course, fresh croissants to go with it. If you prefer to sit down to eat rather than stand at the counter, expect to pay extra. In some bars and cafes, you need to collect a voucher (*scontrino*) for what you want from the cashier before ordering; in a growing number of cafes, however, you simply order, eat and then ask for a bill before you leave.

A welcome cappuccino

Lunch is usually eaten in either a cafe, *ristorante* or *trattoria*. Never judge an establishment's cuisine by its appearance – the best food is often served at the most modest-looking restaurant. Light snacks are also available pizzerias, grills or *Tavola Calde*, and *paninoteche,* which serve *panini* – toasted sandwiches that make for a good lunchtime snack.

Before dinner in the evening, it is the custom to take an aperitif, of which there are countless different types, from alcohol-free versions (*bitter analcolico*) to the highly popular *Campari*. Beer can be obtained everywhere but is rather expensive; local wines (*vino locale*) are better value. Mineral water (*acqua minerale*) is popular and is availabe fizzy (*gasata*) or non-fizzy (*naturale*).

Milanese cafe

The Italian custom is to eat at least two or three courses: a starter such as Parma ham and melon, followed by a pasta dish or rice dish (*risotto*) as a first course (*primo*), then a second course (*secondo*) of meat or fish, accompanied by vegetables or salad (for a range of popular dishes and Milanese specialities, *see page 90*). If you still have room, this can all be followed by one of many mouth-watering desserts (*dolce*), cheese (*formaggio*) or fruit (*frutta*).

If you don't think you manage such an amount of food, you should be allowed to eat just as many courses as you want to. Italians often round off their meals with an *espresso*, sometimes laced with a dash of *grappa* or brandy (*caffè corretto*). An alternative is to drink an *amaro* (*digestif*), of which there is a vast selection. A cover charge (*coperto*) will often be added to the bill; service may also be added.

Italian fruit and vegetables

Restaurant sign

Milanese specialities

Bresàola: Dried and smoked fillet of beef, eaten either cold (marinated in oil and lemon juice) or hot (fried with parsley, garlic, onions and herbs)

Busecca: Tripe soup with chopped parsley or beans.

Cassoeula: Pork, pig's trotter, sausage and cabbage stew.

Costoletta alla milanese: Breaded escalope of veal.

Minestrone alla milanese: A kind of vegetable soup; eaten hot in winter, and either hot or cold in summer.

Ossobuco: Leg of veal cut into thin slices, cooked lightly with bone marrow and tomato purée and served with *risotto*, mashed potato or *polenta* (maize porridge).

Risotto alla Milanese: Rice cooked in saffron and stock.

Stufato: Beef pot roast with a lot of herbs and spices.

Zuppa pavese: Hot meat soup with toasted bread, egg and grated cheese.

Panettone: light sponge cake, typically eaten at Christmas.

Popular cheeses include Gorgonzola, Mascarpone, Stracchino, Grana (similar to Parmesan), Robiola, Taleggio, Fontina and Bel Paese.

Good local white wines include: Franciacorta Pinot, Lugana, Tocai di Lugana, Trebbiano, Riesling and Cortese. Reds include: Sassella, Grumello, Inferno, Valgella, Botticino, Cellatica, Riviera del Garda, and Quistellese.

Restaurants

Below is a selection of restaurants. Those in the centre are marked with a (C), those near the station with an (S) and those near the exhibition centre with an (E). Prices are guides only and are for dinner for one, excluding wine.

LLL: around L90,000
LL: around L60,000
L: around L30,000

Gourmet restaurants

The following serve expensive gourmet cuisine, both classic Italian and international, and some Milanese fare.

Biffi Scala Toula, Piazza Scala (C), tel: 02-866651. Stylish twists on classic cuisine; some Venetian dishes. **LLL**

Il Teatro, Four Seasons Hotel, Via Gesù 8 (C), tel: 02-77081435. Creative, sophisticated, light cuisine in a former convent; open for dinner only. **LLL**

Savini, Galleria Vittorio Emanuele (C), tel: 02-72003433. A stuffy but famous spot serving classic cuisine. **LLL**

Peck, Via Victor Hugo 4 (C), tel: 02-876774. Updated Italian cuisine in elegant, modern setting. **LLL**

Milanese cuisine

Bistrot di Gualtiero Marchesi, 7th floor, Rinascente department store, Via S Raffaele (C), tel: 02-877120. Fine views over the Duomo; Milanese and classic menus. **LLL**

Boeucc, Piazza Belgioioso 2 (C), tel: 02-76020224. Typical Milanese dishes in a grand palazzo. **LLL**

Don Carlos, Grand Hotel et de Milan, Via Manzoni 29, (C), tel: 02-723141. A Milanese institution in the city's most historic hotel, this restaurant is popular for late dining, possibly after a performance at la Scala. Subtle classic Italian dishes as well as Milanese specialities. Dress smartly. **LLL**

El Brellin, Vicolo Lavandai, off Alzaia Naviglio Grande, tel: 02-58101351. Converted mill in the canal quarter, serving Milanese food accompanied by live piano music. **LL**

The canal quarter

Regional restaurants

Caajunco, Via Stoppani 5, tel: 02-2046003. Sicilian seafood. **LL**

Al Girarrosto di Cesarino, Corso Venezia 31 (C), tel: 02-76000481. Tuscan cuisine in an elegant setting. **LL**

La Tana del Lupo, Viale Vittorio Veneto 30, tel: 02-6599006. Venetian cuisine in a cosy setting, often to the tune of live harmonica music. **LL**

Also recommended

Capolinea, Via Ludovico Il Moro 119, tel: 02-89122024. Dine late in the fashionable jazz and blues club/restaurant in the trendy canal quarter. **LL**

Orient Express, Via Fiori Chiari 8 (C), tel: 02-8056227. Chic theme bar and restaurant in the style of the famous train. Live piano music. Also serves brunch. **LLL**

Trattoria 23 Risotti, Piazza Carbonari 5, tel: 02-6704710. Offers every type of *risotto* imaginable. **LL**

The ideal lunch

Inexpensive Pizzerie

Premiata Pizza, Alzaia Naviglio Grande 2, tel: 02-894 0648. Pizzeria with courtyard in the lively canal area. **L**

Malastrana, Ripa di Porta Ticinese 65, tel: 02-8378984. Another pizzaria with a courtyard – this one is good for late dining. Smaller than the above but more authentic. **L**

Confectioners – Pasticcerie

Biffi, Corso Magenta 87 (C). Wonderful traditional cakes.
Cova, Via Montenapoleone (C). A chic establishment.
Peck, Via Spadari 9 (C). Tea rooms and a good delicatessen.

Ice cream parlours – Gelaterie

Grasso, Via Cellini 1 (C) and Via Andrea Doria 17 (S)
Odeon, Piazza Duomo 2 (C)
Gelateria Ecologica Artigiana, Corso Porta Ticinese 40 (canal district).
Rachelli, Via Lorenteggio 41
Cremeria Buonarroti, Via Buonarroti 9 (E)
Pozzi, Piazzale Agrippa 4

Italian ice cream is superb

Designer accessories

Shopping

The fashion metropolis of Milan invites a browse along its well-known streets with their most elegant of shops: Galleria Vittorio Emanuele, Via Manzoni, Via Montenapoleone, Via Spiga, Corso Matteotti, Via Dante, Via Mazzini, Piazza Duomo, Piazza San Babila, Corso Europa, Corso Vittorio Emanuele II. In Via Montenapoleone and its side streets one comes across the names of Milan's most famous fashion creators and designers: **Ungaro**, **Gucci**, **Ferragamo** (M Napoleone), **Valentino** (S Spirito for womenswear, M Napoleone for menswear), **Ferrè**, **Versace**, **Krizia**, (della Spiga), **G Armani**, **Trussardi** (S Andrea, with **Emporio Armani** in Durini) and many more. However, there are also more reasonable and less exclusive shops and department stores around the Cathedral Square. The main shopping streets are to be found right at the centre of the city (Corso Buenos Aires, Corso di Porta Romana, Corso Vercelli).

Fashion throughfare

Stylish womenswear

Milan is the capital of Italian publishing, and each publishing house runs its own bookshop. They include **Feltrinelli** (Via Manzoni 12) and **Hoepli** (Via Hoepli 5), the latter being the largest bookstore in Italy. **Galleria Vittorio Emanuele** is home to many bookstores, most of which are also open on Sundays (including Rizzoli and, for art books, Bocca).

The ultimate in Milanese gastronomy can be purchased at **Peck**, Via Torino, and **Il Salumaio**, Via Monte Napoleone. Meanwhile the biggest concentrations of antique shops can be found around the Brera and in the side streets off Via Monte Napoleone.

Markets

Very typical of Milan are the traditional markets, known as the *mercatini all' aperto* and *mercatini comunali*.

Traditional markets include the antiques and bric-a-brac **Fiera di Senigallia**, held all day Saturday at the Darsena di Viale D'Annunzia. On the last Sunday of the month the **Mercatone dell'Antiquariato**, a kind of Milanese folk festival, is held along the Ripa Ticinese and the Navigli Grande. Although it is hard to imagine, even in the 1970s, Milan had the third largest port in Italy in terms of tonnage, and barges used to travel into the city along these navigli.

Every third Saturday of the month (except August) the **Mercatino dell' Antiquariato** is held in Via Fiori Chiari in the Brera. Handbags and jewellery stalls appear here every evening to tempt people out for an evening stroll.

The *mercatini comunali* are held in various quarters of the city and there you can find food, household equipment, fish, etc. These markets are very popular with the Milanese, not least because of the very reasonable prices (try the Saturday market on Viale Papiniano).

A large antiques and flea market, the **Fiera degli Oh bei, Oh bei**, traditionally takes place on 7 and 8 December around the Basilica di Sant' Ambrogio.

For book-lovers, there is the **Vecchi Libri in Piazza**, which is held every 3rd Sunday every month, except July and August, in the Piazza Diaz.

93

Art Nouveau antiques

Getting There

By plane

The nearest airport to Milan is **Linate** (10km/6 miles east of the city); however, since the lengthy refurbishment and expansion of the city's other airport, Malpensa, Linate has been used mainly for domestic Italian flights. **Malpensa** (40km/25 miles northwest), now Milan's principal international airport, is connected to Cadorna Railway Station by the Malpensa Express train service (tel: 02-40099260); the service runs roughly every 30 minutes from 6.30am to 1.30am (5.20am–10.50pm from Cadorna to Malpensa). Tickets cost around L15,000 one way and L20,000 return. A taxi ride from Malpensa to the centre of Milan will cost around L100,00 one way.

British Airways (www.british-airways.com), their low-cost subsidiary airline Go (www.go-fly.com), British Midland and Alitalia (www.alitalia.com) each operate several flights a day to Milan from London. Alitalia offer daily direct flights from the New York to Malpensa.

If you are flying from the UK and planning on visiting the Italian Lakes, another option is to fly by the budget airline Ryanair (www.ryanair.com). Planes fly from London Stansted to the small airport at Brescia. This small town is about 80km (50 miles) from Milan and on the main train line between there and Venice.

By rail

If travelling from the UK, the most direct way is to take the Eurostar to Gard du Nord in Paris, then cross to Gare du Lyon for overnight services to Milan. Anyone arriving by train in Milan will arrive at the Central Station (Stazione Centrale), Stazione Garibaldi, Stazione Lambrate or Stazione Piazza Duca d'Aosta. Metro lines 1, 2 and 3 will then take you into the centre and to the Piazza del Duomo. If you're leaving Milan, remember that you must frank your ticket in the yellow ticket machine at the entrance to the platform before boarding the train; failure to do this is likely to result in a fine.

The platforms at the Central Station are up on the first floor, where you can also find Travel Information (tel: 02-72524360/70), a bank (Banca delle Comunicazioni, open Monday to Saturday 8am–2pm), an automatic currency exchange, several boutiques, a 24-hour pharmacy, a self-service restaurant (11.30am–10pm) and a supermarket (7am–midnight). The tourist office (APT, open 8am–7pm) is on the same level, off the departure lounge. The Albergo Diurno ('day hotel', open 7am–7pm, closed Wednesday) can provide you with a quiet room, luggage service, a bar, hairdresser, 24-hour dry-cleaning service and showers. There is a post office on the ground floor.

Stazione Centrale

By car

In keeping with its importance as an economic centre Milan is served by an extensive motorway network (A1 = *Autostrada del Sole*; A4 = *Serenissima*; A7 = *Autostrada dei Fiori*; A8 and A9 = *Autostrada dei Laghi*, as well as the ringroad *Tangenziale Ovest* and *Est* (*see page 96*).

Visitors coming from Switzerland can approach Milan by motorway via Aosta, Sesto Calende, Chiasso and Como; those travelling from Austria can head over the Brenner Pass to Verona. There are toll charges on all motorways in Italy.

The Azienda Trasporti Municipali (ATM), the municipal transport system, has a series of supervised car parks along the major arterial roads leading into the city. Elec-

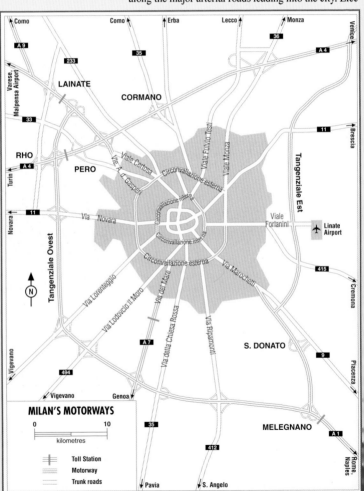

tronic sign boards give information on the nearest car parks and how many places are left. Thus anyone arriving via the motorways or major roads can park his or her car safely at the various public transport termini (eg of the *metropolitana* Metro system).

A driving licence and vehicle-registration documents, a warning triangle and country stickers are compulsory. The international green insurance card doesn't have to be shown at the border but is advisable in case of accident; comprehensive cover is recommended. The following speed limits apply to motor traffic in Italy unless otherwise indicated: 50kmph (30mph) in built-up areas, 90kmph (55mph) on country roads, and 130kmph (75mph) on motorways (*autostrada*). Speed limits are often lowered at weekends or on public holidays. Police checks have become much stricter in recent times, and excessive speed as well as excessive alcohol consumption can cost motorists their licence – this also applies to foreign drivers. Seat belts are compulsory in Italy.

The number to ring in case of breakdown in Italy is: 116. The SOS emergency number is 113.

Heed warnings

Getting Around

Parking

A complicated one-way system only allows entry to the city at certain points (and restricts access to the centre). Obtain a zonal map from a car hire or tourist office. Parking in a central blue zone requires a *SostaMilano* disc (purchased from bars or *tabacchi* kiosks displaying the ATM sign as well as selected Metro stations); unlawfully parked cars get towed away. Should this happen to you, ring the police *(vigili urbani)* on 02-77271 and ask for *Uffizio*.

The ubiquitous scooter

Public transport in Milan

Maps of Milan can be obtained from stations, airports, newsagents, kiosks, from the tourist information centres in the Central Station and Via Marconi 1, and from the city transport office (ATM), in the Duomo Metro station directly beneath the Cathedral Square. *Page 98* shows a map of the Metro system and the names of the individual stations. The Metro runs until from 6am until about 12.30am.

A single ticket *(biglietto ordinario)* currently costs L1,500 and is valid for 75 minutes of travel on all types of public transport (Metro, tram, bus). These tickets need to be bought in advance from automatic machines (drivers don't sell them), and stamped when entering buses or trains. They are available at news kiosks in Metro stations and also from various bars. Tickets are available from ATM offices and tourist offices. There are convenient day tickets valid for 1 or 2 days for tourists who want to make full use

Travel by tram

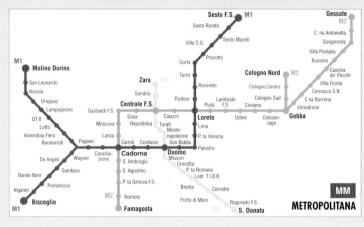

of the system. Children taller than 1m/3ft 3in need tickets; only collapsible prams can be taken onto the metro.

Taxis

The majority of taxis in Milan are now white, although you may still see some of the older yellow ones. Taxis, which are relatively expensive, should be taken from any one of the many taxi ranks in the city. Individual cab ranks can also be contacted by phone (consult the phone-book for their telephone numbers). For radio-taxis, dial 02-5353, 02-6767, 02-8383 or 02-8585.

Taking the bus

Hire cars

These are available from the Stazione Centrale and from Linate and Malpensa airports, as well as from Hertz (tel: 02-6690061), Eurodollar (tel: 02-66710104) and Avis (tel: 02-6690280) amongst others. Further information on car hire is available from the APT and all major hotels.

Bus and tram tours

From Tuesday to Sunday the travel agency Autostradale organises bus tours of Milan, which leave from in front of the Palazzo Reale at the south side of the Cathedral and last 3 hours, taking in all the major sights. Reservations can be made in several Milan travel agencies and at the tourist office (tel: 02 72524301/2/3)

In addition, there is a tram tour of the city. Tram Turistico (tel: 02-8055323), which leaves several times a day from Piazza Castello. You can buy tickets on the tram; audio commentary in Italian, English, French and German. It is a 'hop-on hop-off' tour that takes from 1 hour 45 minutes to all day. Tickets valid for the whole day.

Details on a combination bus/boat tour – the major sights by bus followed by a trip along the canal Naviglio Grande – can be obtained from the APT, Via Marconi 1.

Facts for the Visitor

Visas

Visitors from European Union countries require either a passport or identification card to enter Italy. Holders of passports from most other countries do not usually require visas for a period not exceeding three months.

Milan coat of arms

Customs

If you are an EU visitor, there are no duty-free limits, provided that whatever you buy is for personal use. If you bring back more than the following guidance levels for consumer goods, customs may ask you to prove that the goods are for your own use: 800 cigarettes, 200 cigars, 1kg of tobacco, 90 litres of wine, 10 litres of spirit and 100 litres of beer per person.

Information

Information can be obtained from the offices of the Italian State Tourist Office (ENIT) at the following addresses:

In the UK: Italian State Tourist Office, 1 Princes Street, London W1, tel: 020-7408 1254; fax: 020-7493 6695.

The main tourist office **99**

In the US: Italian Government Tourist Office, 630 5th Avenue, Suite 1565, NY 10111, New York, tel: 212-245 4822; fax: 212 586 9249.

For tourist information in Milan you should contact the provincial tourist information offices known as the Azienda di Promozione Turistica (APT). These are open all year round: Palazzo del Turismo, Via Marconi 1, tel: 02-72524300; fax: 02-72524350 (summer: Monday to Friday 8.30am–8pm, Saturday 9am–1pm, 2–7pm, Sunday 9am–1pm, 2–6pm; winter: Monday to Friday 8,30am–7pm, Saturday 9am–1pm, 2–6pm, Sunday 9am–1pm, 2–5pm); Piazza Duomo; Stazione Centrale; Airport.

Information sections listing the events of the coming week (theatre, cinema, concerts, etc) are included in the Wednesday edition of the Italian daily paper *Corriere della Sera* and the Thursday edition of *Repubblica*. Also useful are *A Guest in Milan* or *Hello Milano*, available from major hotels, and *Milano Mese* (in English and Italian) from the tourist office.

Money, banks and exchange

Exchange welcome

The unit of currency in Italy is the lira (abbreviated to Lit. or L). Since the introduction of the euro on 1 January 1999 some shops quote prices in euros as well as lire.

Banks are generally open Monday to Friday 8.30am–1.30pm and 2.30–4.30pm. The bank at the railway station is open every day from 8am–7pm. B*ureaux de change* are open every day until 7 or 8pm. Most credit cards, including Visa, Access and American Express, are accepted in ho-

tels, restaurants and shops and for air and train tickets and cash at any bank. There are numerous automatic teller machines ('Bancomat'), which commonly take Visa, Mastercard, Cirrus and Maestro.

Bills and Tipping

Restaurants are required by law to issue an official receipt to customers. Confusingly, although most restaurants include VAT *(IVA)* in the bill, service *(servizio)* may be extra and, in grander places there tends to be a cover charge *(coperto)*. Even if you see the words *Servizio compreso*, a small tip is expected. Check the menu carefully.

Opening times

Remember that many shops and most museums, churches and filling stations close for lunch. Smaller shops are generally open from 9am–12.30pm and from 3.30–7.30pm. Large department stores, supermarkets and many of the shops in the city centre remain open all day.

Around 15 August, the time of *Ferragosto*, many shops, bars and also museums are closed. Those open are listed in the daily papers or in the *Hello Milan* monthly guide.

Opening hours for the major museums are given in this guide (most are closed one day a week – usually Monday). For more information contact the APT.

Public holidays

1 January (New Year); 6 January (Epiphany, or *Befana*); Easter Monday; 25 April (Liberation Day); 1 May (Labour Day); Ascension; 15 August (Assumption of the Virgin, or *Ferragosto*); 1 November (All Saints' Day); 7 December (Sant'Ambrogio, only in Milan); 8 December (the Immaculate Conception); 25–26 December (Christmas).

The Italian postal system

Post

Milan's Posta Centrale (main post office)is at Via Cordusio 4. Stamps *(francobolli)* can be purchased from post offices and tobacconists *(tabacchi)*. Post boxes, which are red, usually have one slot for internal Milan post and another one for everywhere else.

Telephoning

Nearly all phone boxes work with phone cards *(carta telefonica)*, bought at tobacconists or news-stands. Some phone boxes also take cards and 100, 200 or 500 lire coins.

To call abroad, dial 00 then the country code: Australia 61; France 33; Germany 49; Japan 81; Spain 34; United Kingdom 44; US and Canada 1. If calling Milan (even a local call within the city) note that you must still dial the 02 code; if calling from abroad, the '0' from 02 is retained. For directory enquiries, dial 12.

Time
Italy is six hours ahead of US Eastern Standard Time and one ahead of Greenwich Mean Time.

Voltage
Usually 220v, occasionally 110v.

Medical
With an E111 form from the Department of Health and Social Security, UK visitors are entitled to medical treatment in Italy. It is, however, still advisable to take out travel insurance. Holiday insurance policies are recommended for non-EU visitors.

Theft
Carry valuables close to your body and keep a firm hold on handbags. All cases of theft need to be reported immediately to the police *(Carabinieri)*; call their stolen-goods department *(Questura)* on 02-62261.

Emergency numbers
Police: 112
SOS Emergency Number: 113
Fire Brigade: 115
Ambulance: 118
Emergency Medical Aid: 02-3883

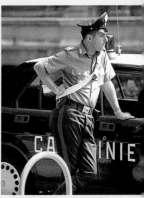

Ask a policeman

Lost and found
The city's *Ufficio oggetti rinvenuti*, Via Friuli 30 (tel: 02-5465299), is responsible for objects lost on trams, buses or Metro trains (Monday to Friday 8.30am–4pm, closed Saturday and Sunday). Another lost property office (Via Sammartini 108, tel: 02-67712677, open daily 7am–8pm) is responsible for objects lost on trains or in the station.

Consulates & Embassies
British Consulate, Via San Paolo 7, tel: 02-723001.
US Consulate, via Principe Amedeo, tel: 02-290351 (for visas 02-29035280).

Useful websites
- www.autostrada.it (official motorway website)
- www.fs-on-line.com (official Italian Railway site)
- www.inlombardia.it (general site on Lombardy)
- www.meteo.it (the weather in Italy on-line)
- www.museionline.it (Italian museum site)
- www.teatro.it (Italian theatre site)
- www.ticket.it (ticket reservation in Italy on-line)
- www.vivamilano.it (general Milan site)
- www.ambitalia.org.uk (Italian Embassy/Consulate site)
- www.enit.it (official Italian Tourist Board web page)

Hotel Principe di Savoia

Accommodation

The official rating

Milan is well provided with superior hotels but has few decent hotels below 3-star. Hotels are mostly set in the centre, especially around Piazza della Repubblica and the Central Station, with others near La Fiera, the trade-fair centre. During fair periods *(see page 7)*, hotel rooms are in short supply so book ahead. Contact the hotels directly or call an agency such as Milano Hotels Central Booking, Piazza Missori (tel: 02-8054242/56; fax: 02-8054291) to book. You can also visit: www.traveleurop.it.

Milan's official hotel categories can be misleading – always check whether breakfast and taxes are included in the price and if weekend/non-fair rates are available. The ranges below (for a double room) are given as guides only.

5-star and luxury hotels
(L500,000 and above)

Four Seasons, Via Gesu 8, tel: 02-770881; fax: 02-7708 5000. Set in a 15th-century convent in the fashion district, the Four Seasons is considered to be the city's best hotel. Relaxed, country-house atmosphere; impeccable service.

Grand Hotel Duomo, Via San Raffaele, tel: 02-8833; fax: 02-86462027. Wonderful central location overlooking the cathedral. Lovely roof terrace. Recently redesigned.

Meridien Gallia, Piazza Duca d'Aosta, tel: 02-67851; fax: 02 66713239. The restored, period-furnished Gallia is one of Milan's top hotels. Home to the Canova Restaurant.

Principe di Savoia, Piazza della Repubblica 17, tel: 02-62301; fax: 6595838. This is a grand, old-fashioned alternative to the Four Seasons. Roof-top gym and pool.